If from your first meeting with a woman
you remember her dress, it means it was
an ugly dress; if you remember the woman,
it means that she had a beautiful dress.
Coco Chanel

RotoVision

A RotoVision Book

Published and distributed by RotoVision SA
Route Suisse 9
CH-1295 Mies
Switzerland

RotoVision SA
Sales and Editorial Office
Sheridan House, 114 Western Road
Hove BN3 1DD, UK

Tel: +44 (0)1273 72 72 68
Fax: +44 (0)1273 72 72 69
www.rotovision.com

10 9 8 7 6 5 4 3 2 1

ISBN: 978-2-88893-008-2

Art Director for RotoVision: Tony Seddon
Design: JC Lanaway
Cover illustration: Robert Brandt
Typeset in Univers and Akzidenz

Printing and binding in China by Midas Printing Ltd.

Issues

6 **What is Fashion Design?**
Fashion versus clothing
Identity
Art or fashion?

18 **The Fashion Story**
The rise of the designer
Twentieth-century fashion
 revolutionaries

38 **Fashion Communication**
Fashion and cinema
Fashion magazines
Fashion shows
Fashion photography
Fashion and the internet

44 **Fashion as Big Business**
Global economics and fashion
Luxury brands and empires
The democratization of luxury

52 **Fashion and Celebrity**
Celebrity endorsements
Celebrity designers
Celebrity ranges for retailers

58 **Fashion Ethics**
The body beautiful
The fur debate
Eco fashion
Workers' rights
Ethical supply chain

Anatomy

66 **Fashion Segmentation**
Haute couture
Ready-to-wear
Diffusion lines
Sportswear
Tailoring and modern menswear
Mass-market fashion

78 **Trends and the Zeitgeist**
The zeitgeist
Trends and fashion forecasting
Textile trade exhibitions
Fashion stylists
Fashion editors

86 **The Fashion Calendar**
The fashion cycle
The production calendar
Collections and ranges
The role of fashion weeks

96 **From Sketch to Dress:
the Design Process**
Who are you designing for?
Research and investigation
Research sources
The muse
Collating research
The importance of drawing
The silhouette
Proportion, line, and balance
Color and fabric
Design development
Putting together a collection and range
Presenting design proposals
The toile

118 **Careers in Fashion**
College and university courses
The entry portfolio
What to expect on the course
The exit portfolio
Life after graduation
Setting up an independent label

Portfolios

128 **Portfolios**
130 **Viktor & Rolf**
140 **Boudicca**
148 **Rei Kawakubo**
    (Comme des Garçons)
160 **Walter van Beirendonck**
172 **Hedi Slimane**
182 **Zac Posen**
192 **Marc Jacobs**
206 **Duckie Brown**
216 **Rick Owens**
232 **Derek Lam**

Etcetera

246 Glossary
248 Resources
254 Index
256 Credits

What is Fashion Design?

Fashion versus clothing

Whether consciously or unconsciously, fashion and clothing play important roles in our daily lives. The simplest routines of getting dressed in the morning, whether for work, pleasure, or even the gym, require us to make decisions on how we present ourselves to the world and what might be comfortable and appropriate for any given task. When we buy clothes, we again engage ourselves in a decision-making process: is this color too bright? Can I wear this for work? Does it make me look fat? While interacting with peers, visiting shopping malls, flicking through magazines, or watching movies and television, we are overwhelmed by an array of styles, colors, and shapes. This daily contact becomes a vehicle in building a relationship with clothes, helping us to make decisions and informing our judgment.

Informed by these concerns, anthropologists, philosophers, psychologists, sociologists, theorists, and academics alike have brought the subject of dress, clothing, and fashion to the forefront of modern culture.

With ever-expanding markets, which inevitably increase the variety on offer, what actually differentiates "fashion" from "clothing"? In simple terms, "clothing" can be described as something that covers and protects the body. Function takes precedence over style or aesthetic form; color, fabric, and details rarely change. The local climate, terrain, and cultural and social values also play important roles in determining dress. Utility clothing, such as uniforms and workwear, is designed with the prime purpose of protection and practicality. From time to time, due to rebranding or a breakthrough in technologically advanced fabrics, the requirements, color, fabric, and style of utility clothing might change. However, the alteration will be modest and the primary aim remains functional.

Fashion, on the other hand, is usually presented twice yearly, as spring/summer and fall/winter collections. It is led by fast and continual changes of style, materials, and details. In comparison with the functional and basic nature of clothing, style reigns supreme.

The primary function of fashion is to deliver, season after season, an up-to-date look or trend to the consumer. This may sound fickle and pretentious. However, fashion dress has complex underlying characteristics, more than just what first meets the eye. Designers work hard to connect with the consumer on an aesthetic and emotional level. Subject matters such as sexuality, identity, gender, and conceptual form are often discussed via fashion dress, catwalk presentations, and the fashion media. Designers also look to history and historical dress, different cultures, politics, economics, and technology for their inspiration. Alongside their biannual fashion collections, designers collaborate with stylists to present new hair shapes and lengths as well as new make-up looks for the season. The aim is to entice the consumer to buy products and be part of the ideal fashion package.

Identity

What we wear and how we wear it helps to express individuality, a visual form of free speech. Dress can also affiliate the wearer to a particular group with similar thoughts, likes and dislikes, origins, cultures, or religions. Ancient civilizations and cultures from Asia, Africa, and the Americas practiced forms of adornment such as tattooing, body piercing, body painting, and the wearing of animal skins and feathers to express individuality, affiliation, and status. Likewise, since the 1940s, youth cultures or style tribes in the West have influenced generations and helped individuals to associate themselves with like-minded people. Each group is characterized by its particular dress code, musical tastes, and political and social values. Universally recognized are the teds, skinheads, rude boys, punks, mods, new romantics, and goths. A more recent group, b-boys and flygirls, emerged from the ghettoes of New York with their distinctive rap music and break dancing. Their style became a medium for young African Americans to tell the world about life in the ghetto.

Dress can also help to signify symbolic recognition. This could be religious, including a particular ceremonial dress, or it could be occupational. Within both, differentials are commonly found to help define and segregate rank and authority. The ancient Romans commonly used dress to show social divisions: slaves had long hair and did not shave, whereas freed slaves shaved their hair and wore a cap called a "pileus" as a mark of distinction. Roman citizens, although not forbidden to do so, rarely wore

hats. Only the emperor wore an imperial crown—a solid gold wreath of laurel leaves—reaffirming his status and authority. To this day, royalty display their status by wearing heavily adorned garments and jewels on formal or state occasions.

Many societies and cultures traditionally wear symbolic dress to mark important occasions such as marriages and deaths. Interesting differences can be found between cultures; for example, in the West it is common for a bride to wear white at her wedding, as a symbol of purity and virginity, whereas in many Asian cultures a bride is heavily adorned, wearing bright colors, usually red, as a sign of celebration. In stark contrast, white is the color worn by widows of all ages.

Uniform is the obvious form of occupational dress, worn by institutions such as the police, the army, and emergency rescue crews. The uniform displays the wearer's affiliation to an organization, and also helps an individual to stand out in a crowd. Uniforms symbolize power, authority, and rank, both within society and within an organization itself.

Fashion and dress can also help to define gender and sexuality. The term "androgyny" relates to gender ambiguity and the mixing of feminine and masculine characteristics. In the 1920s and 1930s, a community of lesbians living in Paris dressed in masculine attire to openly advocate their sexuality. In the 1970s, the gay liberation movement took a similar approach, although rather more radical and less subtle, to express their sexuality. Many lesbians had crew cuts and wore flannel shirts and heavy work boots. Gay men showed their feminine side by experimenting publicly with make-up and drag. By the 1980s, androgyny had spread into mainstream culture. Male rock and pop stars such as David Bowie and Boy George crossed gender lines by adopting big hair and heavy eye make-up, while singer Annie Lennox wore severe, cropped hair and masculine-looking suits.

In 1965, Yves Saint Laurent created a seminal moment in fashion. Drawing inspiration from the history of lesbian cross-dressing in Paris, as well as the contemporary trend toward androgynous dressing among young men and women, he created the female tuxedo, which he called Le Smoking. By feminizing the basic shapes of the male wardrobe, Saint Laurent set new standards in fashion. He not only adapted the male tuxedo for women, but also safari jackets, brass-buttoned pea jackets, and flying suits.

Previous page:
Alexander McQueen
McQueen was known for his dramatic, thought-provoking, and subversive portrayal of fashion. Here he presents his vision of the crucifixion of Jesus Christ within a fashion context on the catwalk.

Right: Raf Simons
Menswear designer Raf Simons introduces an ultrafeminine silhouette for fall/winter 2008. Simons has become famous for questioning male identity and playing with the notion of a "fourth sex."

Art or fashion?

The close relationship between art and fashion has existed for centuries. For a long time the relationship was one-way traffic; artists used fashion in their paintings and sculptures as a way to depict society. Not until the Renaissance did fashion, as a medium, play a stronger role. Artists such as Antonio Pisanello (c. 1395–c. 1455) not only portrayed fashion in their paintings, but also actively designed textiles and embroidery.

The modern era has seen designers and artists flirt ever closer with the notion that fashion is about more than just dress and appearance. The boundaries that once may have existed between art and fashion are now blurred. The understanding of art and its characteristics has allowed designers to explore and portray highly charged moments of emotion, sexuality, gender, politics, modernism, and romanticism, and project an array of semiotic and subversive messages, whereby the wearer becomes a walking canvas.

In the early twentieth century, avant-garde movements across Europe expressed their beliefs through fashion. Influenced by the British Arts and Crafts movement, the Weiner Werkstätte (the Vienna workshops), made up of artists, architects, and designers, fused together the aesthetic ideals of art and design. Inspired by functional objects, they produced furniture, glassware, tableware, and ceramics alongside their practical vision for fashion. Their style of work was characterized by a play on unusual color schemes and colorfully contrasting designs, featuring geometric shapes, stripes, and small stylized flowers.

Although they did not innovate new garment shapes or silhouettes, their original and accomplished use of color influenced many independent artists and designers unconnected to the Weiner Werkstätte, such as Sonia Delaunay (1885–1979). Trained and working as an artist in Paris, Delaunay was renowned for her interpretations of Orphism, a form of abstract painting with affinities to Cubism. A strong believer that color was a primary means of expression, she was able to create a visual flow by contrasting blocks of color with geometric designs on fabric. Her considerable impact on how art and fashion could overlap was further highlighted by her idea that the cut of a garment should be conceived in conjunction with the textile design.

Stefano Pilati
Pilati, creative director of Yves Saint Laurent, recreates a modern version of the legendary androgynous look, Le Smoking, at Paris Fashion Week fall/winter 2009.

Inventive and influential, Delaunay went on to collaborate with Chanel, and designed clothes for movies and the theater.

The Russian Constructivists Varvara Stepanova (1894–1958) and Lyubov Popova (1889–1924) based their fashion on ideology. Their designs combined creativity, comfort, and utility, with the primary aim of reforming the social environment. They were able to explore and practice their artistic beliefs without the constraints of consumerism. Their key design features were based on functionality and simple silhouettes deriving from traditional peasant costume, with detachable pockets and sleeves, zips, and contrasting colors and materials. This led to their fashion being modern and innovative.

Between the two world wars, Surrealism, centered mainly in Paris, led the way for new thinking within literature and the arts. Fascinated with the Surrealist concept of fantasy, fashion designer Elsa Schiaparelli rejected the modernism of the 1920s. She experimented with new materials—plastic, glass, cellophane, parachute silk—and intentionally exaggerated her accessories. Her collaboration with Surrealist artist Salvador Dalí was art and fashion's most iconic partnership of the twentieth century. Dalí designed prints for two of the most talked-about dresses of the 1930s: the Tear Dress and the Organza Painted Lobster Dress. The Tear Dress gave an illusion of tatters and violence and was inspired by one of Dalí's paintings, *Three Young Surrealist Women Holding in their Arms the Skins of an Orchestra*, where torn fabric is impossible to tell apart from torn skin. The Lobster Dress carried with it sexual connotations; Dalí often used the lobster in his works to convey sexual messages. Strategically placed, the lobster at the front

John Galliano
Inspired by the geometric qualities of Russian Constructivism, the renowned referential designer John Galliano presents Dior's 1999 spring/summer prêt-à-porter collection at Paris Fashion Week. His use of color and geometric patterns is in keeping with the ideals and aesthetic of the Russian art movement.

of the dress seemingly climbs toward the wearer's thighs. If the intention was to shock, this was achieved.

The excitement of the 1960s brought with it a new approach to art and fashion. The couture industry was losing its influential hold on fashion due to the demands of the consumer, with a shift in power toward ready-to-wear and mass production. With this in mind, Yves Saint Laurent designed a collection of wool jersey tunic dresses inspired by the Dutch abstract painter Piet Mondrian, which came to be dubbed the Mondrian Look. Simple in cut, without the fuss of couture, the dresses featured intersecting black lines and blocks of bold primary colors. Saint Laurent used the abstract and geometric qualities of Mondrian's paintings to great effect, using the dresses as his canvas. In 1966, again inspired by art, he designed a collection based on the principles of the Pop Art movement and its most celebrated artists, Roy Lichtenstein and Andy Warhol. The collection was made up of vibrant, cartoonlike motifs depicting mass culture and consumerism.

During the latter part of the twentieth century, art and fashion continued to morph together. Advancements in photography and its acceptance as an art form contributed to the cementing of this relationship. Photographers have exploited fashion for its subversive and semiotic qualities, and the fashion industry is now able to expose and promote a designer or a label as a brand like never before.

Fashion is a prominent part of modern culture, and film, photography, shop window displays, and installations have become part of the canvas on which fashion paints its picture. Fashion now sits comfortably within art galleries, which were previously exclusively home to paintings, installations, and sculptures. Global exhibitions dedicated to fashion and retrospectives of fashion designers are now commonplace. As past and present art depicts culture, society, and the human condition, the same can be said for fashion; pushing ahead producing biannual depictions of provocative subject matters within a contemporary context, it has become as powerful, if not more so, as art itself.

Yves Saint Laurent
These A-line, Andy Warhol-inspired dresses were made from paper and were meant as throwaway items. The self-indulgent and consumer-led fashion industry fitted in well with Warhol's artistic beliefs and played an important role in the dissemination of Pop Art.

Overleaf:
Hussein Chalayan
Conceptual fashion designer Hussein Chalayan's presentation of his 2001 spring/summer collection at London Fashion Week is more akin to an art installation than a catwalk. Two models chip away at material from a dress, simulating a work-in-progress sculpture.

The Fashion Story

The rise of the designer

Today, top fashion designers enjoy celebrity status and attract loyal groups of followers. Designers use a variety of means to stay in the media spotlight, including catwalk shows that set out to shock, glamorous magazine spreads, and interesting and obscure collaborations. This continuous self-promotion has enabled designers to become brands themselves, giving them a powerful platform for bringing their visions to the forefront of modern culture.

Above and right: Tom Ford
Tom Ford (above) has become an iconic celebrity designer. He is credited with bringing a new super-sexy approach to the Gucci brand. Overseeing everything from menswear and womenswear design to perfume branding, Ford as Gucci's creative director showed how the luxury brand could be promoted and perceived. He himself promoted the very same sexy aesthetic. Shown right is one of Ford's many glamorous dresses, presented at Gucci's fall/winter 2004 catwalk show in Milan.

Jacques Doucet
A typical early 1900s haute couture dress by renowned couturier Jacques Doucet displays elaborate use of fabrics and trims.

The emergence of the modern fashion designer has a humble beginning, which also coincides with the birth of haute couture. Charles Frederick Worth, the "Father of Couture," was born in 1825 in Lincolnshire, England. Working at fabric stores in London and Paris gave Worth an understanding of fabrics and sales techniques, as he learned how to choose and manipulate fabrics to suit customers' personalities and facial features. Worth established his own dressmaking business in Paris in 1858. His "salon" became a haven of creativity and exclusivity. Regardless of status, all clients had to make an appointment to visit the salon. There, the client was presented with the latest styles from the current range. Once chosen, the style was made precisely to the client's personal measurements. This bespoke practice and personal attention between client and creator led to the promotion of exclusivity throughout Europe, reaching as far as the wealthy North American market. At its height, the salon employed 1,200 staff, made up of cutters, seamstresses, hand- and machine-embroiderers, models, and salesmen.

This original way of presenting fashion promoted a signal vision and aesthetic, propelling Worth from the position of a mere dressmaker into a creator of fashion. Following his lead, a number of couture houses were established and a new industry was born. In 1868, Worth founded the Chambre Syndicale de la Couture Parisienne. This body was set up to regulate the standards, quality, and practice of couture houses; it still exists today.

Twentieth-century fashion revolutionaries

Paris from 1900 to 1914 was the epicenter of the luxury industries, which included textiles, jewelry, and fashion. The early part of this period saw little change in the appearance of women. The Edwardian silhouette, the "S" shape with its tiny waist, could not be achieved without being caged in by a corset, which pushed the pelvis back and the chest up and out. Outer garments were indulgent; lace, silk, ribbon, heavy embroidery, brocade silk, and rose trims were used to create a sumptuous and elaborate style.

The maverick Paul Poiret (1879–1944) shocked the fashion establishment by breaking away from these accepted norms. Inspired by avant-garde artists like Picasso, Poiret enjoyed a sensational rise to fame. A talented self-publicist, he credited himself as the man who liberated women from the corset. In 1908 he unleashed his biggest break from convention and introduced a collection called the Directoire, or Empire, line. Skirts fell straight from the waist to an inch or two from the ground, while the waistline rose to just below the bust, eliminating the need for a corset and replacing it with a high-fitting boned belt. Although a major shock to the established system of dress, it only took two years for this new softer line to be universally accepted. Poiret's designs combined a variety of inspirations, including orientalism, art deco motifs, turbans, flowing pantaloons, the exotic geisha kimono, and the everyday peasant dress of Ukraine.

An innovator with a modern approach to marketing, Poiret was the first couturier to launch a perfume; Rosine appeared in 1911, ten years before the iconic Chanel No. 5, and Poiret personally coordinated the fragrance, packaging, and distribution.

As well as being a fashion designer, Mariano Fortuny (1871–1949) was an active painter, sculptor, photographer, and designer of textiles, furniture, and theater design and lighting. He devised special techniques for pleating and dyeing fabrics, and in 1909 took out patents for his dress designs—or, as he saw them, his inventions. Along with Poiret, Fortuny was a leading fashion modernist of the early twentieth century, taking women's clothing into new and uncharted territory of femininity and freedom.

With the outbreak of World War I in 1914, the role of women changed significantly. While large numbers of men were away fighting the war, women had to take over their jobs. As women went to work in factories, they required a new form of dress. Pants, overalls, and dark monochrome colors replaced the overtly feminine ideals of the opulent society of the past.

In 1915, designers introduced practical daywear, influenced by military uniforms. Tailored jackets and suits with gently waisted silhouettes became an important part of a woman's wardrobe. Pockets, which once did not exist, were now a prominent feature, echoing the functional qualities of military uniform. With hemlines creeping up to 2 or 3 inches (4 or 5cm) above the ankle, shoes and boots also became more fashionable.

The French designer Gabrielle "Coco" Chanel (1883–1971) gracefully accepted this new attire, in keeping as it was with her

Coco Chanel
Christian Dior said of Coco Chanel, "With a black pullover and ten rows of pearls, she revolutionized fashion."

modernist aesthetic of simple line, form, and function. Ridiculing designers such as Worth and Poiret for their overelaborate creations, Chanel set out to change the face of women's fashion forever.

The inventor of "poor chic," Coco herself was the muse, designer, and the attitude. Inspired by men's clothing, she revolutionized the use of jersey knit, which until then was used only for men's underwear. Her first collection, La Pauvrete de Luxe in 1916, placed no emphasis on the waist, where it had been for centuries. The Chanel vision had no place for padding and corsets; outfits were understated, simple, and sporty. Her ruthless sense of line and proportion and her obsession with perfection were to stay with Chanel throughout her career. Buying into the Chanel vision meant that women were encouraged to make choices for themselves and what suited them, as opposed to following fashion slavishly. The emphasis was on comfort and clothes that felt like a second skin.

The aftermath of World War I saw women change in more ways than one. In Britain and the United States they had the vote and they were out of corsets, giving them a newfound physical and symbolic freedom. Waistlines dropped dramatically, hemlines rose above the knee—uncovering legs for the first time in history—and dresses were sleeveless and backless. The hint of nudity and sense of the risqué were heightened by the use of delicate, gauzy fabrics. "Flapper" dresses echoed the new flat-chested, boyish, body shape that women now yearned for. Hair, once a woman's crowning glory and a symbol of her femininity, was cut into a short Eton crop.

Chanel continued to make fashion headlines throughout the 1920s. Already inspired by the male wardrobe, she introduced men's blazers, shirts, and jackets to womenswear, often using thick tweed and wool to characterize the androgynous look. As if this weren't radical enough, she also introduced yachting pants, which she often wore herself, accelerating the move toward women wearing pants.

The creation of Chanel's legendary "little black dress" in 1926 has become a seminal moment in fashion history. American *Vogue* likened it to the Model T Ford car and called it "Chanel's Ford... a uniform for all women of taste." Chanel endorsed the color black, feeling it could be exploited for its elegance and its capacity to flatter. It may have changed over the years, but the little black dress is still authoritative and designer collections are rarely without a version of this ageless design classic.

As Chanel pioneered the La Garçonne look, Madeleine Vionnet (1876–1975) found her inspiration in the timeless beauty of Greek statues, and her liberation of the female body took a different approach. An architect of dress, she invented the bias cut, a method of cutting garment patterns by placing them diagonally at a 45-degree angle. Vionnet's technical prowess not only unshackled the female form, but also accentuated it through brilliant drapery. The bias cut, cutting across the grain of the material, enabled fabric to flow and cling into folds and shapes. Those who saw Vionnet working up her preliminary designs on small dolls likened her to a sculptress creating modern neoclassical dresses. Vionnet's sensitive approach to the female form cemented her reputation in fashion history, and her bias cut technique still inspires contemporary designers such as John Galliano and Azzedine Alaïa.

The stockmarket crash of 1929 led to a worldwide depression and mass unemployment during the 1930s. The French haute couture industry, dependent on export trade to the United States, took drastic measures as orders from department stores and private buyers were cut or cancelled. Prices were slashed and cheaper ready-to-wear ranges and fashion-related products were introduced. Labor-intensive techniques such as embroidery were abandoned in favor of establishing form and silhouette. Unlike the boxy, loose shapes of the 1920s, clothes in the 1930s were cut in a more provocative way to follow the lines of the body. The bias cut was now being used to draw attention to every curve.

Cinema helped provide a refuge from the misery of the depression, as Hollywood films and their glamorous heroines offered up escapism and dreams. The relationship between fashion and film had begun. The glamor of Hollywood had an influence on trends, as stylish actresses such as Greta Garbo, Vivien Leigh, and Marlene Dietrich became major silver screen idols.

Throughout the 1930s, beauty and health became increasingly linked. Sports clubs and leisure activities became an important feature of life, and sportswear increasingly appeared in the mainstream, inspiring designers to produce sporty casualwear.

The German occupation of Paris during World War II posed the biggest danger to the haute couture industry, as it faced the threat of being forcibly moved to Berlin and Vienna. With support from the collaborationist French government, the Chambre Syndicale de la Couture Parisienne stood firm and independent, and most couture houses continued to operate. Black-market racketeers and the wives of Nazi officers and foreign ambassadors kept the industry alive. More than 100 couture houses managed to survive and stay open, including Worth, Pierre Balmain, Jeanne Lanvin, Lelong, and Balenciaga, consequently securing about 12,000 jobs.

In a bid to help the war effort, new regulations were brought in governing the clothing industry. Silk was deployed for making parachutes and wool for military uniforms. Manmade fibers such as rayon, synthetic jersey, and nylon were the alternatives. In the United States, regulations were put in place by the War Production Board, whose "no fabric on fabric" rule meant that cuffs and patch pockets were banned.

In Britain, the Board of Trade introduced the Utility Scheme to ensure value for money. The scheme had a stringent code with no unnecessary decoration allowed. A dress, for example, could not have more than two pockets, five buttons, six seams in the skirt, and 160 inches (4m) of stitching. However, through the label Incorporated Society of London Fashion Designers, the Board of Trade proved that the limitations of utility did not rule out style. Leading designers Hardy Amies, Digby Morton,

Bianca Mosca, Peter Russell, Victor Stiebel, Creed, and Edward Molyneux were commissioned to design an all-year collection comprising an overcoat, suit, blouse, shirt, and day dress. Cut, line, and simple elegance were key. The silhouette was narrow and tailored with pronounced shoulders and nipped-in waists. The military influence was inevitable and was seen in belts, breast pockets, high-cut necks, and small collars.

As French couture houses operated under the restrictions of the Nazi occupation, couture and ready-to-wear were flourishing in the United States. Designers such as Claire McCardell (1905–1958), regarded as the inventor of the American casual style and a forerunner to Calvin Klein, became a household name. With the rationing of silk and wool, she turned to cotton, jersey, denim, and mattress ticking to produce mix-and-match separates that were uncluttered, easy to wear, and inspired by the functionality of sportswear.

When Christian Dior (1905–1957) presented his first collection in 1947, dubbed the New Look, there was shock, horror, and outrage along with the excitement of a new dawn. Leaving the austerity of the war behind and putting regulations aside, Dior tempted women back into the femininity of corsets and, most controversially, flowing skirts that used 50 yards (45m) of luxury material. Pulled in by an undergarment called a "waspie," waists were tiny, while jacket shoulders were narrow and slightly sloping—all perfectly balanced to accentuate the length and fullness of the skirt.

During the 1950s, the House of Dior was responsible for the majority of Paris' exports to the United States. Dior's untimely death in 1957 ended a career that lasted only ten years, and yet this visionary achieved so much. Although his designs were not for mass consumption, they provided a vision for an entire society, setting the standards for beauty and an ultrafeminine silhouette.

While Dior played with a romantic interpretation of the Belle Époque, the work of Cristobal Balenciaga (1895–1972) was strictly modern. A purist and a master cutter and colorist, he achieved perfect line, balance, proportion, style, and palette through his technical prowess. Responsible for numerous forward-thinking silhouettes and styles, he invented the three-quarter-length sleeve and the standaway collar. A master of illusion, he had the ability to make the neck appear long and slender by revealing the clavicle, and making the wearer appear taller by pitching the waistline just above the natural level.

Christian Dior
Haute couture evening
dresses by Christian Dior. The
hourglass silhouette typified
Dior's "New Look," which
caused a sensation on its
launch in 1947.

Postwar America was flourishing as economic and industrial advancements put it in a commanding and influential world position. Inheriting this new global position, a generation of young, affluent, and liberated Americans were now being recognized as a distinct social group: teenagers. With their new spending power, teenagers were able to cultivate their own looks, fashion, and identities, rejecting the rigid conformity of their parents' generation. Movies and music had a big impact on youth culture, bringing through new looks and also rebellious, antifashion attitudes. Transatlantic travel and improved communications helped to disseminate these trends and attitudes around the world.

The influence of Hollywood meant that screen beauties dictated notions of beauty, sexuality, femininity, and style. Marilyn Monroe and Brigitte Bardot popularized the curvaceous and provocative look, whereas Grace Kelly and Audrey Hepburn were classic and sculptured. Hepburn became the inspirational muse for the French couturier Hubert de Givenchy. He designed clothes for many of her movie appearances, and she also wore his clothes off-screen.

The emergence of America saw Parisian couture lose its supremacy. The new consumer society, together with technological breakthroughs in synthetic fabrics such as rayon and nylon, proved to be an enormous catalyst to America's fashion industry, laying the foundations for today's industry. Ordinary American women still wanted the diktats of Paris fashion, but without the costs. Manufacturers and retailers were quick to realize this demand and bought the original rights from Parisian designers. The clothes were then copied stitch for stitch, so that women could buy quality, ready-to-wear Parisian-style fashion in American department stores.

The haute couture business in Paris was still supported by a small band of loyal clientele, but on the whole the industry was in decline. While couturiers continued to strive forward with beautifully crafted designs, the cost of labor-intensive custom design outweighed the decreasing profits. Mass production, the growing ready-to-wear market, and the teenage revolt had a direct effect on business. In order to survive, the couture houses introduced new marketing techniques and luxury goods to secure their immediate and future existence. Dior had already foreseen the advent of new markets and had diversified into stockings, lipsticks, and other accessories. Others soon followed with ready-to-wear lines, perfumes, and make-up.

Hubert de Givenchy
The little black dress that Audrey Hepburn wore in the 1961 film *Breakfast at Tiffany's* has become a fashion icon, epitomizing the understated, refined elegance of Givenchy's designs.

By the mid-1960s, the fashion pendulum had swung once more, this time in favor of Britain. London's Carnaby Street and Kings Road—the centers of British ready-to-wear—represented the optimistic times and a youthful style to the rest of the world. Unlike the extravagance and expense of Paris, London's philosophy was based on high fashion at inexpensive prices. Designer Mary Quant—credited with the invention of the mini skirt, skinny rib sweater, and false eyelashes—became synonymous with the "swinging sixties" in London. To capture the feeling of freedom and innovation, she reinvented the use of an industrial material called PVC and designed a collection called the Wet Look. Art schools in London became creative havens for innovation, nurturing designers such as Zandra Rhodes, Bill Gibb, and Ossie Clark.

Ossie Clark, in collaboration with his wife, textile designer Celia Birtwell, produced fashion that brought together print designs with technical and creative cutting in a perfect marriage. Clark's heavily choreographed fashion shows were revolutionary, featuring models dancing down the catwalk to music played by DJs. Each show was a spectacle in itself, laying the path for fashion shows as we know them now.

Although London was now the creative hub and fashion leader, Parisian couturiers Pierre Cardin, Paco Rabanne, André Courreges, and Emanuel Ungaro averted the demise of the French haute couture industry by producing collections for the ready-to-wear markets. Inspired by space exploration and futuristic innovations, they used new techniques for construction, fabrics, colors, and accessory designs.

By the end of the decade, however, fun and optimism had given way to depressing political events. With the daily news diet of the Vietnam War, Watergate, race riots, and student protests, the world was now looking a very different place. The same youth who were once setting the agenda in the utopian 1960s were now antiestablishment. This cynical mood created an antifashion attitude, seeing it as superfluous. However, fashion remained a strong vehicle for expression, though it now took a very different style. The 1970s saw the baton passing from London to San Francisco, the birthplace of hippie culture advocating free love and peace. Customized flared blue jeans, Indian scarves, afghans, flower-print tunics, ankle-length maxi skirts and dresses, long hair for girls and boys, and cheap accessories summed up the look of this antifashion movement preoccupied by dreaming of a happier future.

American black soul music became popular, bringing with it a radical chic influenced by Angela Davies, James Brown, and Diana Ross. Disco fever gripped America and Europe, influencing a sexier, more fluid silhouette. American designers Halston, Bill Blass, and Oscar de la Renta caught the moment, transposing this sexier look to American women. American fashion on the whole saw a new establishment of designers coming through, staking an independent aesthetic.

As ready-to-wear flourished on both sides of the Atlantic, Balenciaga, the great master couturier, declared the end of haute couture

Sixties swinger
Young British model Twiggy
came to symbolize the
"swinging sixties" in London.

and shut down the couture side of the business. Yves Saint Laurent was now the torchbearer for Parisian fashion and was given star billing by all major fashion editors. Ostentatious and sensational, he was in tune with youth trends and movements. Saint Laurent sent out models in men's suits, with the aim of freeing women from the trappings of feminine, frilly dresses. The masculine suit remained a reoccurring theme for Saint Laurent throughout the 1970s, also influencing designers such as Karl Lagerfeld at Chloé and Ossie Clark.

Suffering from economic decline, Britain in the late 1970s saw the emergence of the antiestablishment and antifashion punk scene. The Sex Pistols, managed by Malcolm McLaren, together with designer Vivienne Westwood, established the punk look with bondage pants, kilts, and T-shirts with provocative imagery. Worn with boots, chains, leather jackets, and spiky, multicolored hair, the look was finished off with an array of safety pins and body piercings. Individual and opinionated, this was the voice of anarchy. London-based textile and fashion designer, Zandra Rhodes, created contemporary versions of the look that were more conventional and were accepted by a wider audience.

The decade may be generally remembered for platform shoes, flares, hippies, punks, and altogether bad taste. However, it is important to remember that the 1970s was an era of real self-expression, when dress and fashion were not only about displaying a particular look, but also an attitude and political belief.

The 1980s was altogether a different decade; this was a boom period and consumerism was once again king. Status symbols and designer labels became a necessity: Filofax personal organizers, Mont Blanc pens, Rolex watches, Louis Vuitton luggage and bags, Chanel jewelry and handbags, and Porsches represented the money-oriented society. In the field of fashion, there was also a shift toward an expensive and flamboyant look. In this media-saturated climate, clever marketing and PR techniques turned designers and models into celebrities.

Women were asserting themselves in the male-dominated office environment, so "power dressing" was a must for every career-minded woman. The suit became more versatile than the little black dress; wide shoulders accentuated the narrowness of the hips and the skirt was short and tight. Designers also experimented with bright primary colors, animal prints, geometric patterns, stripes, and dotted prints. And if this weren't enough, an array of fabrics such as leather, tartan, and silks were deployed to assist the extravagance.

Karl Lagerfeld, now artistic director of Chanel, reworked the famous Chanel suit in different fabrics, colors, and accessories. French designer Thierry Mugler took the suit to a new level. Mixing futurism and Hollywood retro, his designs were overtly sexy and fetishistic. The silhouette was characterized by broad shoulders and a defined waist. With a similar design aesthetic to Mugler, Claude Montana was among the most talented young Parisian designers. Figure-hugging designs in leather and lightweight fabrics were created for his vision of a galactic heroine. Broad shoulders, nipped-in waists, and robotic detailing became his hallmark.

With most designers preoccupied with the suit and the extravagant silhouette, Azzedine Alaïa took advantage of DuPont's new fabric, Lycra. Alaïa's designs defined the Lycra revolution, bringing the emphasis clearly back to the female form. His collections embodied the sex appeal of the 1980s, selling out within days of their arrival in stores.

In 1983, the avant-garde designers Rei Kawakubo and Yohji Yamamoto left the international fashionistas with their eyes and mouths wide open—they had just witnessed the Japanese revolution. Breaking away from the prevailing image of the polished femme fatale with an accentuated waist, broad shoulders, and killer heels, they offered a black, sculptured, deconstructed alternative. Kawakubo's subversive collection introduced a new silhouette that included coat dresses cut big and square, made from distressed fabrics with misplaced necklines and collars. Models were devoid of any lacquered prettiness; instead they displayed a bruised blue on their lower lips. The fashion press saw the collection as a political statement and dubbed it the Post-Hiroshima Look. Yamamoto also introduced a radical approach toward the female form. Oversized, draped, and ingeniously cut garments wrapped around the body, creating moving human sculptures.

Issey Miyake, the third element of the Japanese triptych, also embraced modernist visions. He made innovations in materials, leading him to explore garments with a new perspective.

Still feeling the after-effects of a conspicuous consumer society and the boom-and-bust economy of the late 1980s, the 1990s had a gloomy start. There was a huge backlash against the values of the 1980s, which inevitably filtered through into fashion. The music of Seattle-based rock bands Nirvana and Pearl Jam influenced the grunge look, a combination of punk and hippie styles. The look was interpreted by American designers such as Marc Jacobs and refined by Donna Karan, Ralph Lauren, and Calvin Klein. The latter found the perfect model to present this style: with her waif-like image and stunning beauty devoid of any artifice, Kate Moss became the face that personified the decade and the Calvin Klein brand.

In Britain, John Galliano and Alexander McQueen recaptured the rebellious spirit of British fashion. With the personal backing of American *Vogue* editor Anna Wintour, Galliano presented a collection in Paris in 1993. At the time, he was financially broke, had no backing, and this was his last chance. Using only leftover black lining fabric, he presented a collection that was exquisitely cut in the traditions of haute

couture. This collection became a defining moment in fashion history. Sitting in the front row was Bernard Arnault, chairman of the LVMH group, which owns Givenchy and Dior. Witnessing the magic of Galliano, Arnault made him creative director at the House of Givenchy in 1995, and two years later, he was handed the golden shears—the reins at Dior. Galliano has never looked back.

In 1995, McQueen's politically charged Highland Rape collection referenced the plunder of the Scottish Highlands at the hands of the British gentry. He displayed his skills as a technical and creative craftsman, and also his ability to shock. He was later given the role of creative director at Givenchy, filling the void Galliano had left. McQueen was a rebellious genius, whose work often provoked and amazed. Tragically, he took his own life in 2010.

The success of Galliano and McQueen started a trend for traditional fashion labels to be rejuvenated by new blood. Chloé appointed Stella McCartney, while Julien MacDonald designed knitwear for Chanel while still a student at the Royal College of Art; he later became head of Givenchy. American designers also had a strong presence: Tom Ford brought sex appeal back to the Gucci label, and for a brief spell at Yves Saint Laurent; Michael Kors went to Celine, Marc Jacobs to Louis Vuitton, and Martin Margiela to Hermès. Fashion was now big business and brand identity and market share were key to success.

As London and Paris jostled for supremacy, a new breed of designer, one that had first emerged in the late 1980s, was now making its mark. This was to be the Belgian revolution. Known as the "Antwerp six," Dries Van Noten, Dirk Bikkembergs, Dirk Van Saene, Ann Demeulemeester, Walter Van Beirendonck, and Marina Yee brought with them a whole new gritty and perfectionist attitude. Despite their shared training in the fashion department of Antwerp's Royal Academy, their individual styles remained distinct and varied.

Fashion in the 1990s sparked off a new revolution of design aesthetics and designers willing to go that extra bit further to shock, provoke, and provide new shapes and forms. No real trends were established as in previous decades: skirt hems were long, short, and asymmetric; colors were bright, tonal, and subdued. Astute marketing and promotion has helped designers establish themselves, and perfumes, make-up, accessories, and diffusion lines are now part of every successful label. Today, ready-to-wear is the new haute couture. Haute couture has become a business tool, a promotional model for the house to promote its products and cheaper ready-to-wear lines.

Ann Demeulemeester
Ann Demeulemeester typifies what is now recognized as the "Belgian Look." Her twenty-year reign as the queen of underground rock-heroine style has made her an icon.

Left: Yohji Yamamoto
This piece from Yamamoto's fall/winter 2009 Paris ready-to-wear collection illustrates the Japanese designer's unconventional approach to the female figure.

Right: John Galliano
This collection for the fall/winter 2009 Paris ready-to-wear show was inspired by Russian and Balkan folk costumes.

Fashion Communication

Fashion is all about communication: it transmits an ideal, an aesthetic, a style, and an attitude for the consumer to buy into. Investing in advertising, photoshoots, fashion shows, boutique interiors, and endorsements helps to establish, cement, and promote the brand identity. The importance of these key marketing and advertising exercises can be measured against multimillion-dollar budgets.

Successful communication involves creative practitioners from parallel industries, such as photographers, movie producers, magazine editors, and stylists. Concepts are created in collaboration with fashion brands to communicate a brand identity that can influence a generation, change cultural and social attitudes, and create iconic moments and trends.

Fashion and cinema

Since the advent of cinema, movies and fashion have worked closely together. Fashion provides filmmakers with an ideal way to communicate character and identity, and to suggest a social context. And film, with its cinematic sequences, stills, and sense of drama, is a perfect idiom for fashion to be experienced. The power of film and its ability to reach a wide audience has made it a profitable medium with which the fashion industry can promote its product.

Credited with designing the original "It" look and making it popular, English couturiere Lucile was one of the first established designers to venture into film in 1916. She was soon followed by the likes of Elsa Schiaparelli and Chanel. However, it is the partnership of Hubert de Givenchy and Audrey Hepburn that has become famous for its perfect balance of timeless elegance, style, and glamor, in line with the master couturier himself. Movies such as *Sabrina*, *Funny Face*, and *Breakfast at Tiffany's* have become influential fashion movies the world over, setting global trends and responsible for the Audrey Hepburn look being copied by millions of women.

Originally designed specifically for workwear, the humble white T-shirt and jeans can attribute their success and longevity to James Dean in his lead role in *Rebel Without a Cause*. The look has become a timeless classic for both men and women, and has been interpreted by different designers in their own distinct way. It is moments like this that give movies and fashion the authority to influence a generation and challenge the social framework.

More recently, the relationship between fashion and movies has created a new genre of film. As well as mainstream movies with a fashion theme, such as *The Devil Wears Prada*, younger and more avant-garde fashion labels together with video artists are writing, producing, and directing their own arthouse films. Examples include *Office Killer* by Cindy Sherman, *Fashionnashion* by Ruben Toledo, *Treason—Dress Code* by Sergei Pescei and Patricia Canino, *Chapels—Bernhard Willhelm* by Diane Pernet, and *The Bridegroom Stripped Bare* by Alexander McQueen. Exhibitions and festivals have been created to show this work and encourage people to experience a new intellectual and artistic link between fashion and film.

Fashion magazines

Magazines are an integral part of the fashion industry, helping to publicize trends, sell beauty and fashion products, and promote designers and labels. The magazine industry is one in which the fashion designer has little say or command—the editor rules. The success of a collection is dependent on the level of coverage the editor wishes to give it. Impressing the right editors can guarantee overnight success and bring recognition to an unknown designer, but can also lead to a premature downfall if a collection fails to impress.

Magazines such as *Vogue* and *Harper's Bazaar* are the torchbearers and have remained in prominence while others have come and gone. *Vogue* started business in 1892, and from its conception it has remained in the forefront of the fashion press. It introduced the use of fashion illustration, and prominent artists and illustrators Paul Iribe, Erté, and Barbier pioneered the style of fashion drawing in the 1910s and 20s. Taking inspiration from theater, interiors, and decorative arts, they helped to idealize the representation of a fashionable world. As photography became more popular, *Vogue* and others were able to communicate in a more sophisticated way. The medium allowed magazines to express fashion within a wider social and cultural content.

In the 1980s and 90s, British magazines such as *The Face*, *i-D*, and *Dazed & Confused* were launched to feed an audience concerned with street style and popular culture. Taking on a distinct style of fashion journalism, these magazines have an urban, underground, and gritty quality. Offering a hybrid of music, film, dance, politics, and fashion, these magazines provide raw footage of fashion in contrast to the glossy spreads of mainstream titles.

Fashion weeklies, such as *Grazia*, have had a great impact in recent years, providing a mainstream audience with a glossy magazine that provides fashion coverage with a celebrity bias. Together with celebrity gossip, how to achieve designer looks at affordable prices are a main feature. Cheap and intellectually accessible, magazines such as these have become very popular.

The magazine industry is highly competitive. Magazines depend on commercial advertising revenue to exist, and the downfall of the global economy in the late 2000s has meant that advertising revenues have decreased. Inevitably, magazines are finding it more difficult to survive and stay in business. The successes of online magazines and websites have provided stiff competition and have challenged the existence of the fashion magazine as we know it.

Fashion shows

The fashion show as a spectacle is now an integral part of the fashion industry. It gives a fashion label an undiluted opportunity to convey its design identity and vision for the coming season.

From humble beginnings and low-cost productions, the fashion show has become more like a movie set, and the production teams are nearly as big. Disused railway stations, hospital wards, airplane hangars, lavish banqueting halls—whatever the space, it can be transformed into a theater of artistic dreams, fantasies, and daring sensationalism. All of this helps to drill the core design statement through to the press, buyers, trend scouts, and those who disseminate the look into mainstream fashion. However, this level of show production is the reserved luxury of the haute couture, ready-to-wear industry and for newly formed independent labels that receive financial backing via commercial sponsorship.

Smaller-scale shows also take place in shopping malls, boutiques, and department stores. Although less formal and not as intense, they serve a similar purpose—to help reaffirm to customers what and how to wear a new collection and show potential consumers the latest looks and trends, including accessories, make-up, colors, and fabrics.

Fashion photography

In the early part of the twentieth century, fashion photography was seen as a simple way of delivering fashion on a page. In the 1960s, fashion photography broke from convention by applying radical new approaches in methodology and storytelling. However, it was not until the early 1970s, when the work of Guy Bourdin and Helmut Newton drew attention to the aesthetic values of imagery, narrative, and process, that attitudes toward fashion photography shifted and it came to be seen as a legitimate creative process and art form in its own right.

Fashion photography is now a fully fledged industry, and collaborations between stylists, make-up artists, and fashion designers are common. Together, via poetic or satirical use of imagery, fashion photography is able to question and put forward views on morality, sex, gender, beauty, artifice, seduction, and culture.

Editorial exposure has led to global recognition, elevating the fashion photographer into a cult figure. Notable collaborations between photographers and designers include those of David Simms with Raf Simons and Nick Knight with Yohji Yamamoto.

Derek Lawlor
Photographer Jojo Ma purposefully creates a naive surreal experience via the nature of the set design, lighting, styling, and model choreography in this shot of a dress by Derek Lawlor.

Fashion and the internet

The demand placed on fashion to remain innovative and return something new is ever-present. The advent of the internet has given the fashion industry a new communication tool to convey its ideas and products on a global scale. From superbrands like Gucci and Prada to lesser-known labels, department stores, and boutiques, nearly all have websites promoting their goods and services.

Visiting websites enables customers to gain product information, have a virtual experience, sign up to mailing lists or special in-store or online offers, open communication via email, and feel less intimidated by the guise of a designer boutique. These online features personalize the fashion experience, allowing the customer to feel they are part of the brand and its philosophy, which in turn sets up a loyal client base.

To those who wish to be part of the fashion extravaganza, websites such as Style.com and Vogue.com have brought the exclusive fashion show into the wider domain. Blogging and Twitter further enhance the fashion experience, helping the discerning fashion follower to remain in the loop 24/7.

The internet has revolutionized the fashion experience and along with it has educated the customer and the spectator. Anybody and everybody has an opportunity to voice their fashion opinion, to become a fashion journalist or a fashion editor, or to launch dedicated websites. New tools and devices such as the Apple iPhone have taken fashion accessibility to a new level, introducing dedicated applications such as Style.com into the palm of your hand.

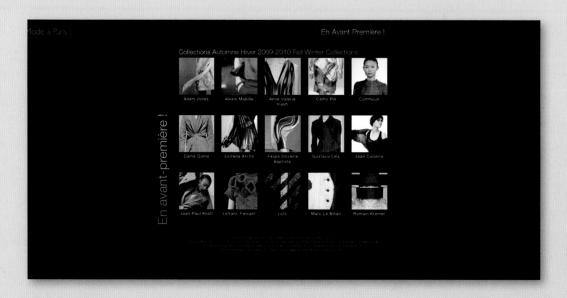

Vogue (left) and Style.com (right)
Fashion websites such as Vogue and Style.com offer readers information on the latest trends, fashion gossip, business news, reports and archives on fashion shows, and beauty tips.

Left: Modeaparis.com
Modeaparis.com provides information about the French ready-to-wear and haute couture industries. It offers designer profiles, press details, and examples of work. This is very much an industry-focused website.

Fashion as Big Business

From unassuming local market stalls selling the basics, bustling malls with designer boutiques and department stores providing extravagant and self-indulgent brands, to shopping via the internet, the fashion industry has become a multibillion-dollar global business. In a market that is highly competitive, intelligent branding and market positioning helps to pinpoint customers and create a desire for consumers to buy into the latest looks.

The term "fashion business" (or "rag trade," as it is sometimes known) is broad and encompasses many different industries. Roughly speaking, the infrastructure can be broken down into the sectors of design, manufacturing, marketing, branding, distribution, and retail. Within this structure, there are many subsidiary industries that link together to form the global fashion chain. For example, within manufacturing there are textile mills producing fabric and factories making component parts such as buttons, zips, and buckles.

In today's fiercely competitive and global business environment, connections and technology are such that a basic T-shirt bought from a local clothing store probably started its journey thousands of miles away. Cotton grown in a field in India or Bangladesh was then spun into a yarn, which was woven into a fabric, which then went to a manufacturer who cut, made, and trimmed the fabric into a garment according to the design specification sheet, which was probably emailed from a design studio somewhere in the West. It is connections like this within the infrastructure that hold the industry together.

Global economics and fashion

As with all businesses, success ultimately depends on sales. Assuming that economic conditions are right and people have disposable income to spend, this produces an upward surge in sales, benefiting the various market segments within fashion. The success of high-volume sales filters through to the local and national economy as well as to the international financial markets, resulting in sustained high employment and wealth within the many industries associated with the infrastructure around the globe.

However, as the boom-and-bust phenomenon of the 1980s proved, a negative downturn in the global economy can be catastrophic. The effects can be felt through all sections of business, and fashion is no exception. Many brands suffered from the 1980s economic fallout—especially those that were already struggling to remain competitive and innovative, such as the Parisian couture houses.

The 1990s, however, was altogether a different era. Political leaders Margaret Thatcher and Ronald Reagan, who were seen as the instigators of boom-and-bust capitalist economic policies, were now out of office; the Cold War ended, and the world was altogether a brighter place. With this renewed prosperity and stability came economic growth and wealth, especially in the equity market. This proved to be the catalyst for the luxury goods market, as economic growth helped to fuel a taste for expensive handbags, shoes, and watches.

Above: Louis Vuitton
Part of the LVMH conglomerate, Louis Vuitton is one of the biggest luxury fashion brands in the world. With flagship stores in all major cities, the LV monogram has become a symbol of the ultimate luxury fashion product.

Overleaf: Prada
The Prada brand has become synonymous with luxury fashion. Under the creative leadership of Miuccia Prada, the company has grown from a reputable leather goods company into a luxury global brand offering a wide range of goods, including ready-to-wear lines for both men and women, watches, jewelry, and bags.

The goods are secondary, because first of all you buy into the brand... you give people the opportunity to live the dream.
Robert Polet, Gucci Group CEO

Luxury brands and empires

In 1987, the merger of two companies, luxury goods brand Louis Vuitton and Moet Hennessy, producers of French champagne and cognac, paved the way for the luxury goods market, including haute couture, to operate in a new and dynamic style.

Within fifteen years, LVMH, as the new company was named, became an international luxury powerhouse. Bernard Arnault, chairman and chief executive, built the world's largest luxury goods empire. LVMH has mercilessly and shrewdly acquired some of the biggest and best-known labels in the fashion and luxury goods sector, including Christian Dior, Givenchy, Celine, Donna Karan, Kenzo, Tag Heuer, Fendi, and Pucci.

The LVMH business model concentrates on four main elements: product, distribution, communication, and price. "Our job is to do such a good job on the first three that people forget about the fourth—price," explains an LVMH executive. For many years, clever branding, advertising, attention to retail ambience, strategic market positioning, and global expansion in network distribution has made the formula work without fault, yielding consistent profit margins of around 40–45% for LVMH's star company, Louis Vuitton.

Prior to 1994, only a handful of luxury goods companies were listed: LVMH, Tiffany, Waterford Wedgwood, Hermès, and Vendome. By the mid- to late 1990s, three names—Richemont, the Gucci group, and LVMH—represented the new global map of luxury fashion. These newly formed conglomerates exerted their financial might and acquired brands that gave them a greater share of the market in haute couture, ready-to-wear, luxury goods, and beauty products. Gucci, once associated with 1970s style and glamor, set out its stall to compete with LVMH and bought Yves Saint Laurent, Sergio Rossi, Alexander McQueen, Stella McCartney, Balenciaga, and Bottega Veneta. Meanwhile, Richemont, predominantly a jewelry retailer, splashed out on brands including Cartier, Chloé, Dunhill, Montblanc, and Bulgari. During this same period, Prada, having launched its successful ready-to-wear label off the back of its handbag specialism, acquired Jil Sander and Helmut Lang.

The designers who came with the fashion houses were regarded as an important part of the package and were tasked to reinvent and transform the brands. LVMH, for example, had John Galliano at Givenchy and in 1997 took him to Dior. Gucci had the super-cool Tom Ford, who later took the helm at Yves Saint Laurent, acquired by Gucci in 2000. Meanwhile, Richemont had Stella McCartney at Chloé. Designers of this caliber not only attracted media attention but became directly associated and representative of the brand identity, serving to intensify the fashionable "must-have" image of the goods.

By 2000, the market was at its peak. LVMH reported first half profit increases of more than 30%. Prada reported a 57% increase, while Gucci's profits rose by nearly 20% in the third quarter. However in 2001, following 9/11, conditions changed suddenly and the bottom began to fall out of the market. The effects of an unsteady stock exchange, layoffs on Wall Street, and bonus cuts began to represent itself in a downturn of sales within the luxury goods market.

The conglomerates suffered a severe drop in profits. Brands that were bought on impulse at overinflated prices were now eating into the profits and costing millions to ensure survival. 9/11 had negative implications for every financial market, but especially for luxury goods, where 30% of the market was dependent on Japanese tourism (Japanese visitors stopped flying to the US in the wake of the attacks because of fears over the security situation). As with the 1980s financial downturn, brands needed to find new directions.

The Gucci group found it hard to compete in the harsher economic conditions and, with its desirable portfolio, lost its autonomy in 2004 to PPR (Pinault-Printemps-Redoute), a French holding company. Decisions were quickly made to redefine Gucci's portfolio position. Out went Tom Ford, and in came young designers to take the helm at some of the biggest brands in fashion. The acquisition of Puma, a leading sportswear company, was a new strategy, opening up a new market share in a sector with huge growth potential.

The credit crisis that began in 2008 also had a negative impact on the fashion industry. The worst economic meltdown since World War II saw the collapse of financial systems, the dissolution of international financial institutions including Lehman Brothers and AIG, and luxury brands Christian Lacroix and Escada filing for bankruptcy. The volatile economic climate has also claimed homes and jobs, feeding insecurity on a daily basis.

In response, independent fashion brands and the big conglomerates had to reevaluate their business strategies to remain competitive. Bernard Arnault, LVMH chairman, suggested that the luxury goods industry rebrand itself. "The word 'luxury' suggests triviality and showing off, and the time for all that has gone," he said. Brands that sold "blingy," easy-to-sell products, milking old names, he believes, will fare particularly badly in the new economic environment. LVMH, by contrast, has never taken this approach, instead emphasizing quality, innovation, and creativity.

Figures suggest that the economic climate has caused consumers to become more discerning, buying products considered to be more of an "investment" for the long term, that are distinctive, classic, and can be worn for years. Therefore, instead of buying three or four pairs of shoes in a season, they might buy just one high-quality pair with classic styling.

The democratization of luxury

Haute couture had been in decline since the end of World War II. Unable to withstand strong competition from young London- and New York-based designers, Parisian couture houses looked into new ways to stay in business, remain competitive, and, of course, make money. The ready-to-wear line was one option that many ventured into. The other was franchising and licensing, which Pierre Cardin took on to expand his portfolio of goods such as watches, luggage, and jewelry. By the beginning of the 1980s, Cardin held more than 500 licenses for all manner of goods. Branching into beauty products and perfume was another route. The brand democratization model was not yet mastered nor fully explored up to this point, and so haute couture continued to have a mediocre existence and luxury goods labels in general remained unknown.

Once a market leader and innovator, Chanel was becoming a tired old brand associated with chic middle-aged French women walking their poodles. However, the appointment of Karl Lagerfeld in the 1980s saw him not only producing sexy and outlandish clothes, but also beginning the democratization of luxury. By taking the mid-1980s "perfume principle" (if you can't afford the dress, you can at least buy the fragrance) a step further, Lagerfeld produced bags, sunglasses, and even jewelry that people who could not afford the clothes could buy in order to be part of Chanel's heritage, glamor, and fashion hierarchy. As the 1990s continued to be financially prosperous, other elite brands inspired by the revolution at Chanel began to remarket and rebrand themselves. With the increase in sales and the growing desire for lower-priced luxury goods, designers such as Giorgio Armani created a diffusion line specifically for those who could not afford his main line collections. Donna Karan, Dolce & Gabbana, Versace, Calvin Klein, and others all followed suit, putting their names to sunglasses, shoes, bags, jeans, and underwear. With Prada's second line Miu Miu in place, the company also introduced their Red Label range in 1998, specifically for consumers who predominately wore sportswear or casual clothing. They therefore increased their market share and competition with market leaders Stone Island and C.P. Company.

While the traditional European luxury houses such as LVMH could not accept offering diffusion or lower-price second lines, they were nevertheless inspired by the media hype, iconic status, and design values of the Prada handbag. LVMH began to increase their luggage range and appointed Marc Jacobs as creative director at Louis Vuitton in 1997. He oversaw Louis Vuitton's first women's ready-to-wear range and gave new direction to the Louis Vuitton handbag. Meanwhile, Galliano at Christian Dior also began to offer contemporary shapes at slightly more contemporary prices, while Gucci refocused on their handbags and shoes. The age of the handbag as a luxury item was born.

People want to belong to certain aspirational worlds. Now, you do it at different price points—somebody buys into this world with a handbag for $500 or $800. And somebody else buys herself a dress for $20,000. Both allow people to be part of the world that they are aspiring to.
Robert Polet, Gucci Group CEO

With levels of disposable income in the 1990s at an all-time high, spending habits among newly wealthy women began to change. The "must-have" culture promoted by seductive marketing and advertising created a swarming frenzy each time a new or limited-edition range was released. No fashion magazine was complete without glossy adverts promoting the latest offerings in luxury handbags, a trend that still continues today. Some women were buying luxury handbags every few months as a display of status and their fashion eliteness.

The success of the luxury goods industry in the last twenty years can be attributed to four main factors: the huge wealth creation of the 1990s; a growth in tourism (newly wealthy people including Chinese and Russians could afford to travel to major cities such as New York, Paris, and London, where they could purchase luxury goods tax-free); increased market share and network distribution by the big fashion conglomerates; and, most importantly, a strategy by the luxury goods houses to foresee the democratization of luxury. It is this last factor that has significantly changed the nature of consumerism as we know it. However, democratization has created a market so fickle and dependent on the economy that anything from a slight dip in the financial markets through to a severe recession sees consumers zipping up their wallets. The very rich are different—they are recession-proof—but they cannot carry the whole luxury goods market alone.

With the success of diffusion lines, mass-market chain stores have jumped on the bandwagon and flexed their financial muscle. As designers try to ride the storm, an opportunity to further their market appeal and share has seen them democratize fashion further down the economic scale. H&M, with its global network of 1,800 stores, took the initiative. Its limited-edition collections have included collaborations with Karl Lagerfeld, Stella McCartney, Roberto Cavalli, Jimmy Choo, Matthew Williamson, Sonia Rykiel, and Comme des Garçons. These have generated favorable media attention as well as a stampede of customers.

Uniqlo
Uniqlo is Japan's largest casualwear brand, with more than 750 stores worldwide. It offers customers the latest fashion at an affordable price. As a result, Uniqlo has become one of the world's leading mass-market brands.

Meanwhile, Alexander McQueen designed a line for the US chain store Target, and Giles Deacon has designed ranges for New Look in the UK. In 2009 there was a highly publicized collaboration between the Japanese casualwear brand Uniqlo and the German designer Jil Sander. The collaboration brought Sander's highly respected design aesthetic together with the financial and distributional might of Uniqlo, which has more than 750 stores around the world.

Once the epitome of budget fashion for the masses, the mall and high street is now becoming the epicenter of democratic luxury, style, and value for money. As financial instability plays its part, luxury boutiques once brimming with rich and aspirational consumers now find the very same aspirational customers flocking to the mall along with the masses to indulge in the new, acceptable face of luxury.

Fashion and Celebrity

In the early twentieth century, fashion designers helped bring about the cult of celebrity by forging a relationship between screen and fashion. In the era of cinema, celebrities were primarily actors and actresses from the silver screen. The original "It" girl, actress Clara Bow, was carefully molded by fashion and Hollywood in the 1920s to represent glamor and style. Other stars such as Gloria Swanson adorned the fashion pages, personifying unrivaled beauty and chic. By exposing and exploiting the celebrity, the fashion industry in return was able to market and promote their latest designs both on and off screen. The affiliation between celebrity and fashion remains strong to this day.

In this era, authors, artists, and sporting heroes also commanded the accolade of celebrity. By the late 1950s, things were

starting to change: rock 'n' roll was taking over the world and the rock star was born. Commanding as much, if not more, exposure through their new brand of music and antics both on and off stage, the rock star was too cool and free-spirited to be drawn into the fashion publicity machine. They remained independent on all fronts, including their fashion and style; they set the trends rather than following them.

In essence, those who were in the limelight had certain qualities; they had excelled within their field or made groundbreaking discoveries. However, the last fifteen years has witnessed quite a cultural shift in the term "celebrity." Being a celebrity now does not necessarily involve having the talent of a sports star, skill of an artist, or the charisma of a rock star or actor. In an era in which privacy is hard to achieve, "reality" magazines and TV shows expose controversial behavior for society to indulge. *InStyle*, *People*, *Look*, *OK*, and *Heat* are just a few of the magazines that are solely devoted to reporting this new brand of celebrity. Born from this are celebrities such who are not known for any particular talent, but rather for their infamy and ability to manipulate and command media coverage.

The glamorous silver-screen heroines of yesteryear now seem like a distant memory. The relationship between celebrity and fashion then was by no means just based on glamor and style; it was status-bearing and had financial incentives for all involved. Nonetheless, in comparison to today's celebrity culture, it seems playfully naive.

Louis Vuitton
Creative director Marc Jacobs chose Madonna to endorse the latest Louis Vuitton bag in this 2008 advertising campaign. The marketing strategy of using celebrities is employed to appeal to a wider audience and drive up sales.

Celebrity endorsements

Actors and actresses provide the perfect scenario for fashion to be endorsed. Millions of moviegoers will see a film; they will experience the clothes, attitude, and style so perfectly portrayed by their screen idols.

A recent example is the New York-based TV series *Sex and the City*, which ran between 1998 and 2004. Based around the friendships of a group of four women, the show became iconic not only for its characterization but also for its influential fashion direction. Each of the four characters had a distinct fashion style that helped portray her personality. Carrie (played by Sarah Jessica Parker) is fearlessly fashionable, her style ranging from uptown chic to whimsical and quirky to sex kitten. Samantha (played by Kim Cattrall) wears sharp styles in bold colors that exude confidence. Charlotte (Kristin Davis) has a sweet, preppy, and demure style with influences from the 1950s. Miranda (Cynthia Nixon) is a well-dressed career woman often seen in smartly tailored suits.

Both the show and the spin-off movies have had an enormous influence on mainstream fashion trends, helping to popularize items such as stilettos, "must-have" designer bags, corsages, and Carrie's distinctive nametag necklace. The casual name-dropping of leading fashion brands such as Manolo Blahnik and Jimmy Choo not only heightened public awareness of those brands but also fostered the aspiration of buying their products. Therefore the connection was forged between fashion product, celebrity endorsement, and viewer.

In today's media-crazed society, celebrities are able to attract attention with minimal effort. This makes them a powerful commodity. Fashion brands have been quick to manipulate celebrity stardom, using them at the height of their fame and paying substantial fees for their association and endorsement. The most successful celebrity–brand alliances match a star whose image is an organic fit with that of a certain brand. In the consumer's mind the two become all but interchangeable. For example, Hollywood actress Uma Thurman is considered to be sophisticated yet unpredictable, the same image cultivated by Louis Vuitton; Michelle Pfeiffer is considered to be mysterious and quietly elegant, reflecting the spirit of Giorgio Armani.

However, endorsements can occasionally go wrong, as was the case for Burberry. In 2005, British supermodel Kate Moss had been chosen to head up a promotional campaign for Burberry, when she made headlines following allegations of drug abuse. Fearful of the adverse publicity, Burberry terminated her contract. Chanel and H&M also followed suit and severed all links with Moss. (Moss' celebrity status quickly recovered, however, and it was only two years later that she began a design collaboration with Topshop.)

As certain brands continue with their celebrity policy, others choose to shun a culture in which they believe fashion has become more about the celebrity than the clothes themselves. The late British designer Alexander McQueen was outspoken in his views on this subject; in 2007 he told US *Harper's Bazaar*,

"I can't get sucked into that celebrity thing because I think it's just crass. I work with people who I admire and respect. It's never because of who they are. It's not about celebrity; that would show a lack of respect for the work, for everyone working on the shows, because when the pictures come out it's all about who's in the front row. What you see in the work is the person itself. And my heart is in my work."

However, the likes of Dolce & Gabbana, Giorgio Armani, Versace, and others of a similar ilk have built their brand identities firmly around Hollywood's A-listers and continue to woo celebrities. More often than not, the front-row seats of their catwalk shows are studded with celebrities, which works as an endorsement in itself. Lesser labels have also followed suit, trying to attract celebrities in the hopes of attracting media coverage and driving up sales. Once upon a time, the front row was made up of fashion press, influential editors, and international buyers—how things have changed.

Celebrity perfumes
Celebrity perfume endorsements have become more popular than ever. Perfume is affordable and for most customers buying a perfume is the cheapest way of being associated with a celebrity or an expensive fashion brand. The launch of Sarah Jessica Parker's own perfume line in an effort to enhance her brand is a commercial tactic pursued by many other celebrities.

Celebrity designers

The mid-2000s saw an unprecedented rise in the phenomenon of celebrities designing under their very own independent fashion labels. This new breed included pop divas such as Gwen Stefani and Jennifer Lopez, rapper LL Cool J, Hollywood star Katie Holmes, socialite Nicky Hilton, Wonderbra model Dita Von Teese, and tennis ace Venus Williams, all of whom launched fashion ranges on the back of their fame. Easily recognizable, they are able to create desire and aspiration, and with constant media coverage the "celebrity" is a brand within itself.

With this level of power and influence, celebrities can go it alone, knowing that they have an eager and ready-made market.

Celebrity ranges for retailers

Shrewd retailers who understand the lure of celebrity culture have in recent years launched ranges in collaboration with celebrity designers. The advantage of this, as opposed to celebrities going it alone in the fashion business, is that retailers have an infrastructure in place, providing financial backing, design assistance, manufacturing, and retail outlets. In return, the retailer gets a famous face to increase sales and improve brand awareness.

In 2007, Kate Moss began a collaboration with Topshop, designing a range of clothing based on her own style of eclectic dressing. Moss has been a controversial figure, but she also has a long career in fashion during which she has adorned fashion and celebrity magazines with her individualistic and influential dress sense. This style has left a lasting impression on teenage girls and women alike, and it can now be bought by those who aspire to the Kate Moss look.

The Kate Moss collection for Topshop was not the first of its kind. It followed in the footsteps of pop queen Madonna, who co-designed her own range for Swedish retailer H&M in 2007. H&M, which has a global retail network, also teamed up with pop singer Kylie Minogue to design a bikini line called H&M loves Kylie.

However, despite the initial hype, celebrity collections and collaborations have come in for some heavy criticism. *The New York Post* in April 2007 declared that the Kate Moss collection "looks like Kate copying a lot of other people's stuff Kate's worn before." Others have called the range "Duplicate" and "Bland."

The future for celebrity collections and collaborations is unclear. No doubt, the marketing ploy has worked in creating a buzz of excitement and streams of customers coming through the doors. However, the failure to impress has led to questions being asked about the products' design authenticity and the celebrity designers' lack of credentials, such as design innovation, technical fashion skills, and invention—qualities that are normally attributed to true fashion designers.

Gwen Stefani
Since 2003, singer Gwen Stefani has been designing for her own range of clothing and accessories called L.A.M.B. The label has been commercially successful and has also been generally well received by the fashion press.

Fashion Ethics

"Fashion ethics" is an umbrella term that encompasses diverse issues such as garment workers' welfare, ecological concerns over the production of raw materials, animal welfare in the fur and leather industries, and the promotion of unhealthy body images. In an era in which there is global concern about climate change and the world's diminishing natural resources, the fashion industry is having to face up to such issues as raised by ethically conscious consumers. The effects of the supply chain, the human costs of production, and issues such as the representation of beauty and body shape on the catwalk and in magazines are just some of the fundamental questions being asked.

More often than not, ethical behavior and responsibility in the fashion industry comes second to the simple facts of profit and loss. For far too long, beauty, glamor, and the all-important "must haves" have taken center-stage in an industry that has raked in trillions of dollars globally. So it is no surprise that ethical issues have generally been met with a blasé attitude from fashion company heads, directors, and executives.

However, new and established designers, fashion press, retailers, and manufacturers have started to acknowledge the conduct of their industry and are finally taking steps to clean up a business that thrives on glamor, fantasy, and controversy.

Fashion magazines are always about some element of fantasy, but what I'm hearing from readers lately is that in fashion, as in every other part of our lives right now, there is a hunger for authenticity. Artifice, in general, feels very five years ago.
Cindi Leive, editor of *Glamour*

Exploited labor
The garment industry often exploits workers in developing countries, using them for cheap labor in sweatshops. Pressure groups such as Labour Behind the Label campaign for workers' rights and better working conditions.

The body beautiful

Whether in a photoshoot or on a catwalk, models often appear as mere clothes horses to display a designer's vision. Magazines, PR agencies, marketing, and stylists all play a part in transmitting such stylized messages. The viewer is seduced and manipulated by these images, which create a need to be part of fashion's flawless world.

However, the effects of such promotional tactics and the pervasive influence of magazines should not be underestimated. A study carried out in the UK probed the extent of the influence that fashion magazines have on their readers. 90% of 11–16-year-old girls read such magazines; furthermore, 80% of women reported feeling worse about their bodies after reading a fashion magazine for only three minutes. Similar surveys have taken place across the Western world and conclude that the influence and glamorization of the so-called ultimate "size zero" body shape has led to an alarming rise in anorexia and other eating disorders, and related deaths.

In the US, "size zero" is an industry-recognized dress size. It represents bust, waist, and hip measurements of 30–23–32 inches (76–60–81 cm), equivalent to a UK size 4 and European size 32. However, the smallest "normal" size for a healthy woman

Above left: Size zero
A gaunt and frail-looking model parades the catwalks of Paris in 2007, highlighting the debate over the unhealthy characteristics of size zero models.

Left: Healthy weight
Matthew Williamson uses the then curvaceous Sophie Dahl as a model for his 2001 fall/winter collection. The question remains, was this just another fashion publicity stunt or a protest against size zero models?

is considered to be a US size 4, representing measurements of 33–26–35in, and size 6, representing measurements of 34.5–27.5–36.5 inches, equivalent to UK sizes 8 and 10. To put size zero into perspective, the average waist size of an 8-year-old is 22in (56 cm).

Magazines have firmly placed the blame on designers and stylists. Their argument is based upon the size of the garments they receive for photoshoots. Over the years, samples have become smaller and smaller, falling from a size 8 to a size zero that has been fitted to the favored "European Ballerina" tall and slender silhouette. In response, designers argue, clothes look better on thinner models because on television and at photoshoots the process of displaying imagery makes the models look bigger. Therefore, bigger models would look even larger.

Together with fashion magazines, the catwalk is also a major size zero offender and promoter. The shocking deaths of former Armani model Ana Carolina Reston and Uruguayan model Luisel Ramos in 2006 revealed the pressure put on models to remain thin and the lengths they will endure to lose weight so they are able to work. Both died from weight-related causes. As a result, Madrid Fashion Week announced in September 2006 that it would ban models with a BMI (body mass index) of less than 18, the lowest weight considered healthy, equivalent to 116lb (52.6kg) for a woman of 5ft 6in (1.67m). In December 2006 the Italian government and the Italian fashion council followed the example, banning ultra-thin models from Milan Fashion Week.

However, fashion bosses in Paris have so far dismissed introducing a ban, while New York's Council of Fashion Designers of America have introduced guidelines to promote healthier behavior, rather than implementing rules on models' weight.

As international fashion show organizers begin to take some responsibility, magazines continue to provide a glamorous and flawless vision of models and celebrities, a proven combination that sells, albeit by artificially raising standards in beauty through retouching, airbrushing, and altering body shape. Concerned with the prevalence of artificially engineered images, leading fashion photographer Peter Lindbergh highlighted the retouching debate by creating a series of front covers for French *Elle* in April 2009 featuring the model Eva Herzigova and actresses Sophie Marceau and Monica Bellucci without manipulation or make-up. The issue struck a nerve with readers in France, where officials have been campaigning for a judicial assessment to force magazines to declare when and how images are altered. Sandrine Levêque, of the women's rights organization OBJECT, welcomed the move by *Elle* by saying, "Initiatives such as *Elle*'s should be welcomed. To see high-profile stars comfortable enough with the way that they look to do that will make other women more comfortable with themselves."

The fur debate

Worn by Hollywood beauties in the 1940s and 50s, fur came to symbolize status and glamor. Fur has lost none of its pulling power and desirability today. It is estimated that around 6.5 million Italian women own at least one fur coat and another 4.3 million dream of buying their first one. For decades, the Italian fashion industry has been a leading producer of fur coats and accessories, employing 56,000 people and producing sales of US$2.2 billion annually to Europe, Asia, and North America.

The desire for fur is opposed by environmental and anticruelty campaigners. In 1994, PETA (People for the Ethical Treatment of Animals) launched a campaign against the use of fur, signaling a major breakthrough in the issue. Supermodels including Cindy Crawford, Naomi Campbell, and Claudia Schiffer appeared naked in adverts with the headline "we'd rather go naked than wear fur." This was the biggest and most potent statement against the use of fur in fashion, and resulted in a decreased number of labels designing collections with fur. PETA's campaign had a major influence and raised much-needed awareness. People in general were more aware and wanted to make a difference. Economically, the move also made good business sense—no fashion label wanted to cause adverse publicity that may have led to a boycott on its goods.

However, a decade later, the very same supermodels who once advocated the ban on fur products publicly turned their backs on the antifur campaign, and once again paraded the catwalks wearing fur designed by Armani, Roberto Cavalli, and Marc Jacobs. With more and more designers choosing to use fur, sales have increased. Statistics from Saga Furs, the main supplier of the world's farmed fur, show that the average age of a fur buyer has fallen from 45 to 35 since 2003, indicating that the youth who once campaigned against fur are now willing to wear it.

Campaigners against fur products remain committed to their aims. Their principle arguments remain the same: they draw attention to the inhumane treatment of animals on fur farms and try to educate the self-indulgent fur wearer who has little or no consideration for the suffering and death of the 54 minks that made up her fur coat. Even though there are now some very good producers of fake fur, this fabric is still widely dismissed by furriers and designers for not having the authentic feel or warmth of true fur. Some 170 designers continue to sidestep the ecological issues and animal rights debate and continue to produce fur goods ranging from coats to purses. However, designers such as Stella McCartney are refusing to cave in to the demands of the luxury fashion industry. A staunch vegetarian, she refuses to use fur or leather in any of her products.

Antifur campaign
American supermodel Cindy Crawford poses naked in one of PETA's early campaigns against fur. She was one of the first supermodels who said no to fur in the 1990s, although, like many others, she is once again wearing it.

Eco fashion

In recent years, consumer awareness and media exposure has shed light on broader global ethical issues. The conscientious consumer now wants to know more about the origins of the clothes they buy.

Climate change and ecological concerns have promoted the use of eco-friendly fabrics. Cotton is one of the world's dirtiest crops when conventionally farmed. It accounts for 16% of global insecticide releases and is responsible for 3 million pesticide poisonings a year, causing 20,000 deaths among agriculture workers. Organic cotton farms are seen as a clean alternative, benefiting both people and the planet. Other alternatives to non-biodegradable, petrochemical-based synthetics include fabrics made from eucalyptus or beech trees, corn, bamboo, and hemp.

Workers' rights

Owing to cheap manufacturing costs, most mainstream fashion production takes place in the developing world in countries such as Bangladesh and Sri Lanka; in recently booming economies such as India and China; and in Eastern European countries such as Romania, Poland, and Bulgaria. China is the leading exporter by far; it accounts for 35% of the world's fashion exports and employs approximately 20 million workers. However, China has become the world's biggest polluter after the US and workers' rights are very limited. Although the fashion industry provides much-needed employment opportunities, lack of workers' rights, poor working conditions, and low wages raise serious questions. Garment workers often live in poverty, sometimes earning just half of what they require to meet their basic needs.

Fashion brands have taken little action even though many of them have signed up to the principle that all workers should earn a living wage. Pressure groups like Labour Behind the Label actively campaign for garment workers' rights in the developing world. Their campaign against Primark in 2007 highlighted the huge profits made by the company in contrast to the poor living and working conditions of the people who manufactured their goods.

Ethical supply chain

Designers can play an important role in creating a more ethical industry. This is not just about choosing eco fabrics; it also involves considering the impact of design decisions further down the supply chain. Ultimately, the problems linked to production are affected by the competitive conditions in the supply chain. The chain includes the production of raw materials, such as wool, cotton, or polyester. These are woven into fabric lengths, dyed, and passed to apparel manufacturers. They cut, make, and trim to a specific design template and then pack, label, and price before delivery to the retailer, who then sells to the consumer.

The demand for "fast" fashion comes at a price: the environment suffers and so do those working in sweatshop conditions. In an increasingly throwaway culture, overconsumption has led to much clothing being discarded after just six months. Now that collections can be put in place in a matter of weeks, new styles and collections are coming and going at a faster pace per season than ever before. "Slow" fashion is the ethical alternative, shifting its emphasis from quantity to quality. It involves designing, producing, and consuming quality-based fashion. It allows for longer lead-in times, enabling suppliers to plan orders, predict the number of workers needed, and invest in the longer term.

People Tree, an eco-fashion label founded by Safia Minney, has stores, franchises, and concessions in Japan and the UK. The company supports 2,000 farmers and artisan communities through fifty fair trade producer groups, in fifteen countries. As well as adhering to a strict environmental policy, People Tree champions organic cotton farming and set up the first organic cotton project in Bangladesh.

Many independent companies are now actively employing ethical principles. As the trends for ethical consumerism increase, so the fashion business is responding. Since 2006, London Fashion Week has hosted Estethica, a dedicated forum for promoting ethical fashion labels. In an environment that hosts avant-garde design and high drama, and where ethical considerations were once ridiculed, both parties now stand side by side. It is cool to be green. However, this raises a serious question: is ethical awareness just another passing trend?

People Tree
This label is a pioneer of fair trade and sustainable fashion. Its products are made to the highest fair trade and environmental standards from start to finish.

Fashion Segmentation

The fashion industry is divided into many parts catering for every taste, budget, and event. This chapter describes the main sectors and gives an insight into their evolution and their working practices.

Haute couture

The term "haute couture" is French. *Haute* means "high" and *couture* literally means "sewing." But the term means much more than just "high sewing"; it has come to represent the exclusive business of designing, making, and selling custom handmade women's clothes. The prestige of such clothing commands the highest prices in the fashion industry, establishing haute couture at the top end of the fashion market.

In 1868, the "father of couture," Charles Frederick Worth founded the union or association of couture houses in Paris—the Chambre Syndicale de la Couture Parisienne. The organization's aims were to ensure quality, to regulate and maintain high standards, retain secrecy, and prevent designs from being copied. New regulations were put in place in 1945 to preserve haute couture's elitist qualities. The regulations were updated again in 1992. These are just some of the directives in place today:

• Designs are made to order for private clients, with one or more fittings.
• The house has a workshop (atelier) in Paris that employs at least twenty people full-time.
• Each season—spring/summer and fall/winter (i.e. twice a year)—the house presents a collection to the Paris press, consisting of at least fifty outfits for both daytime and evening wear.

Members of the Chambre Syndicale must adhere to the strict rules or face disciplinary action or, worse, expulsion. Any new couture houses applying to be affiliated to the Chambre Syndicale must have these measures in place before applying to the executive. Only when members of the executive approve the application is the couture house given the status and the right to label their work "haute couture."

In 1946 there were 106 affiliated couture houses. By 1952, this number had fallen to sixty, largely due to the aftermath of World War II. The world economy was still recovering, and the once-rich patrons of couture were now few and far between. By the 1960s, London's fashion world and the "swinging sixties" had superseded Parisian couture. In this era of youthful rebellion and sexual liberation, the sophisticated, costly look of couture seemed out of touch.

The economic boom of the 1980s and the era of "power dressing" allowed Paris couture to make up some lost ground. This was also a period when multinational conglomerates such as LVMH moved in and bought out some of the long-established couture houses such as Christian Dior. Clothes now became secondary; perfume, cosmetics, and accessories took over, and still remain, as the big money earners.

In 2009 there were only eleven official haute couture houses left in Paris. Although the likes of Giorgio Armani, Valentino, and Elie Saab design couture collections, they are considered part of the second rank of couturiers affiliated to the Syndicale; these are known as "correspondent members." Couturiers of the third rank are known as "guest members," and include designers such as Boudicca and Alexis Mabille. If they are able to meet the strict criteria lay down by the Syndicale, in time such design houses can become part of the elite group that is haute couture.

The significance of haute couture in today's fast-changing world is debatable. The industry has an estimated core clientele of just 2,000, mostly made up of wealthy American women. Is this enough to sustain an industry steeped in tradition and heritage—not to mention prohibitive prices?

Haute couture has now lost its influence to ready-to-wear, and seems unlikely to regain it. However, it has transformed itself into a supremely successful branding and promotional machine for the ready-to-wear, accessories, and cosmetic lines associated with the couture houses. Therefore, haute couture is still in a position to evoke a spectacular fashion fantasy through design and presentation.

Ready-to-wear

"Ready-to-wear" is also referred to by its equivalent French term, "prêt-à-porter." The origins of ready-to-wear may be debatable, but there is no denying the considerable influence of World War I uniform manufacturers, who devised new methods of mass-producing uniforms for the millions of soldiers sent to the trenches. This gave the industry valuable insight into standardizing sizes and led to the invention of new machinery such as industrial presses, electronic cutting tools, and specialist sewing machines. This all helped to speed up the production process.

The most significant difference between ready-to-wear and haute couture is that ready-to-wear clothes are not made to measure specifically for one customer. Ready-to-wear offers the customer the freedom to select garments directly from the rail in various sizes and colorways.

Proenza Schouler
Proenza Schouler present their cool and contemporary ready-to-wear spring/summer 2009 collection at New York Fashion Week. The designers use innovative fabrics and a strong color palette together with strong, uncomplicated silhouettes.

"Ready-to-wear" is an overarching term and can include sectors such as mass-market fashion and casualwear. However, within the fashion industry, the ready-to-wear or prêt-à-porter product is considered to provide high fashion, style, design, concept, and quality. The sector includes designers such as Prada, Ralph Lauren, Calvin Klein, and Comme des Garçons. Unlike haute couture, ready-to-wear labels do not have to be based in Paris and can choose to show their collections during a period known as Fashion Week in New York, London, and Milan, as well as Paris, twice a year (spring/summer and fall/winter).

The demise of haute couture and the rising influence of street style, along with cultural and economic changes such as the social revolutions of the 1960s and the anarchistic 1970s, helped ready-to-wear to become the dominant force in fashion.

Diffusion lines

The term "diffusion line" describes a fashion line from a design house that has been diluted down to imitate its exclusive and expensive couture or ready-to-wear collections at a lower cost and for a wider audience. Early pioneers of the diffusion line included Dolce and Gabbana, who created D&G; Ralph Lauren, who introduced Polo Ralph Lauren and Polo Jeans; Gianni Versace, with its Versace Jeans Couture; and Giorgio Armani, which offers Emporio Armani, Armani Jeans, and Armani Exchange.

Today, nearly all couture and ready-to-wear labels have a diffusion line. The lines are designed to appeal to a broader range of customers; the clothes are cheaper than the main ranges and the line enables the consumer to achieve a designer look on a budget. The tactic is an intelligent branding and marketing exercise; it raises brand awareness, creates brand association, and, most importantly, drives up sales figures. However, the quality and luxury associated with the couture and ready-to-wear lines are not always apparent in the diffusion lines; garments are often made from cheaper fabrics and are mostly mass-produced in factories rather than handmade in an atelier.

Miu Miu
Miuccia Prada presents her diffusion line, Miu Miu, for spring/summer 2010 at Milan Fashion Week. Miu Miu has a younger and more playful design ethos in comparison with Prada's main line.

Sportswear

By and large, sportswear is practical and designed to meet the specific needs of a particular sporting activity. However, cultural shifts in society, the emergence of contemporary popular culture, and radical design innovation has fused fashion and sportswear together to such an extent that at times it is difficult to distinguish between the two genres.

In the early twentieth century, at a time when women were dressed in elaborate and restrictive clothing, liberated women started wearing men's tennis trousers on court, then adopted them off court as a fashion statement. Later, designers such as Coco Chanel and Claire McCardell used jersey fabrics, which were strongly associated with sports attire, to create clothes that were comfortable and allowed greater freedom of movement for women. This opened the door for designers to experiment not only with the design aesthetics associated with sportswear but also its advanced fabric technology.

In the 1980s and 90s, rap and hip-hop musicians from the Bronx of New York and the "soccer casuals" of Britain relied heavily on sportswear brands to create their individual identities. Rappers and hip-hop crews adorned themselves with expensive sneakers, tracksuits, and baseball caps. Until 1986, this look remained confined to the street and with those associated with the music scene. However, when Run DMC had a huge hit with "My Adidas," the look became part of international popular culture. Millions of kids wanted the same look—the sneakers, the tracksuits, and the hoodies. Trendy advertising executives and media moguls from Los Angeles to London also adopted the style. Needless to say, designers took inspiration from this street style and interpreted the look in their way under their own labels.

Meanwhile, in Britain, working-class soccer fans adopted a casual style that mixed traditional British golfing brands such as Lyle & Scott and Pringle, with European sportswear brands such as Fila, Ellesse, Sergio Tacchini, and Lacoste. This sharp style and attention to detail introduced British men to quality European labels. This helped bring about a much-needed revolution in British menswear after an indifferent decade in the 1970s. Up to this day, the soccer casual has remained loyal to the sportswear-branded uniform. Heritage sports brands such as Burberry, as well as high-performance and technological urban brands such as Stone Island, C.P. Company, and Mandarina Duck have become the essential garb of the modern soccer fan.

Sportswear brands such as Nike, Puma, and Adidas have invested heavily in textile and garment technology, resulting not only in increased elegance but also in increased functionality. There are now garments and footwear specifically made for speed, streamlining, to keep the body cool and dry, and to retain body temperature in extreme sports such as mountain climbing. However, as more than 80% of sneakers are bought to make a fashion statement rather than for sports training, sportswear brands have not ignored the financial potential of the fashion market. Prada has produced its Red Label designer sportswear using similar technologies and fabrics, while Adidas and Puma have collaborated with some of the biggest names in fashion.

Adidas, for example, offers Y-3, an exclusive range in collaboration with Yohji Yamamoto that fuses his aesthetic for silhouette with advanced sports technology.

Y-3
Yohji Yamamoto presents his fashion sportswear line, Y-3, in collaboration with Adidas for fall/winter 2009 at New York Fashion Week. The origins of sportswear and contemporary fashion are successfully fused together for a directional and forward-thinking fashion line.

Adidas has also collaborated with Stella McCartney and PPQ. Puma (now part of the multinational conglomerate PPR, which also owns the Gucci group) has offered collaborations with Jil Sander and Alexander McQueen.

The appointment of Hussein Chalayan as creative director in February 2008 gave Puma real fashion authority. "Hussein Chalayan is a proven visionary in the fashion, design and art industries," commented Puma's CEO, Jochen Zeitz; "this would move Puma into a new space, expanding our reach to become the most desirable sport-lifestyle company in the world." Chalayan is responsible for Puma's fashion sportswear line, including footwear, apparel, and accessories.

Sport is a dominant cultural influence in today's world, reflected in our lifestyles and our preference for utilitarian and comfortable clothing. Sportswear and fashion will no doubt continue working together, breaking new technological and aesthetic ground.

Right: Raf Simons
Raf Simons subverts the quintessential male macintosh raincoat by juxtaposing pink sleeves made from neoprene fabric onto a classic body silhouette.

Tailoring and modern menswear

Fashion in menswear has come a long way since the era of the English eccentric Beau Brummell, the revolutionary dandy who broke away from the fancy traditions of men's clothing in the late eighteenth century, which had been dictated by French fashions. Brummell's new, less ornate, way of dressing included woollen fabric instead of silk, velvet, or brocade (this allowed his English tailored jacket to hang impeccably); straight narrow trousers instead of satin knee breeches, and riding boots instead of high-heeled shoes. His style laid the foundations for the English tailoring ethos and cemented the reputation of a community of tailors in London's Savile Row.

To this day, the tailors of Savile Row have been revered for their bespoke, made-to-measure, and handmade garments, which reveal mastery of the tailoring craft. The craft was shaken up somewhat in the late 1980s, when ready-to-wear menswear designers such as Paul Smith, Giorgio Armani, Yohji Yamamoto, and Comme des Garçons became more experimental. They brought in new forms of relaxed and traditional tailoring with a twist, and men were initiated into a new mode of dressing. This had a knock-on effect on the Savile Row tailors, who were still steeped in their traditional bespoke craft and hesitant to follow the trends.

Today, the newer occupants of Savile Row, such as Ozwald Boateng and Richard James, successfully fuse together the traditional and the modern aspects of tailoring. The grand bastions of the craft, such as Kilgour and Gieves & Hawkes, have also moved with the times and now offer off-the-peg collections including suits, leather jackets, and jeans in order to remain competitive.

Away from tradition and the bespoke nature of Savile Row, mainstream menswear design since the mid-1990s has witnessed a phenomenal creative revolution. Designers such as Martin Margiela, Jil Sander, Hedi Slimane (of Dior Homme), Raf Simons, Aitor Throup, Viktor & Rolf, and Bernhard Willhelm have brought about a new order and acceptability, avoiding conformity and the orthodox. Questioning and redefining masculinity, and juxtaposing subject matters such as tradition and street style, grunge and glamor, military and music, and sportswear and tailoring, has led to new and extreme silhouettes, novel garment combinations, experimental fabrics, and bold prints and colors.

Menswear shows have their own dedicated fashion weeks in Milan, Paris, and London (part of London Fashion Week). The new order retains a sense of tradition, but is not a slave to it. Menswear designers remain within the confines of menswear sensibility—men will only go so far.

Mass-market fashion

Mass-market fashion is cheaper than ready-to-wear, but still offers the latest looks. The big chain retailers have become increasingly competitive. They are able to provide a fast turnaround of the latest trends, known as "fast fashion." This is best illustrated in the case of the Spanish retailer Zara, which is able to have a collection on the rail within four weeks from the initial sketch. Their manufacturing and distribution infrastructure is on a very large scale and is highly sophisticated. The clothes are also cheaper due to lower quality of materials, manufacturing processes, and cheap labor costs in cases where manufacturing plants are in Asia. With all these factors put together, they are able to achieve shorter lead times. (The term "lead time" refers to the amount of time it takes from an idea first being seen on a catwalk to it appearing on the market.)

Mass-market fashion retailers can be broken down into different sectors. Stores such as Topshop, H&M, Loehmann, American Eagle, and Zara provide high fashion with reasonable quality. The likes of Primark provide low-budget fashion, everyday clothing at low prices, and low quality. Stores such as Brooks Brothers, The Limited, J. Crew, and Marks & Spencer serve a mature customer looking for fashion consciousness, good quality, and reasonable price. This mixture makes the marketplace vibrant and competitive.

Brands are always looking for ways to increase their market share. Following the diffusion line model, a recent trend has been for major chain retailers and department stores to collaborate with designers to create diffusion lines of their own. The collaborations are seen as offering a taste of the "real" or "authentic" designer's wares, and a step up—unlike the diffusion lines of the ready-to-wear sector, which could be seen as "stepping down."

Another form of mass-market retailing is supermarket fashion. This is not just about cheap, no-frills clothing; branded "supermarket chic" by the fashion press, the everyday basic fashion garments, such as jeans and T-shirts, together with design-

led and value-for-money luxury items such as cashmere sweaters and tailored suits, provide customers with affordable fashion products alongside their groceries and other household items.

In-house design teams for supermarkets tend to pilfer and manipulate current catwalk trends, translating them to meet their market needs and values. Clothing ranges are manufactured quickly and in bulk; therefore, the goods can be sold at competitive prices.

Supermarket fashion continues to evolve, but its fashion concept is somewhat limited due to the nature of its customer base—those millions of savvy shoppers who look out for a stylish bargain while doing their weekly grocery shop.

Zara
Spanish retailer Zara is one of the world's leading mass-market fashion brands. Its appeal is based on its ability to supply fashionable pieces at affordable prices and at a quick turnaround.

Trends and the Zeitgeist

Throughout the twentieth century there have been many fashion revolutions, with designers stimulating new design directions through innovative use of color, fabric, and silhouette. In 1908, Paul Poiret was credited with breaking convention and introducing a new silhouette that did not require women to wear corsets. In the 1920s, designers such as Chanel developed the silhouette further by bypassing the waistline completely and introducing menswear fabrics within her designs, which were inspired by sportswear and the Jazz Age.

In 1947, Christian Dior sent shock waves through the industry with his exciting New Look collection; this was seen as a new chapter in fashion. This was only two years after World War II had ended; not only was the timing of this exuberant collection unexpected, but it went completely against the grain of rationing and the make-do-and-mend mentality, and consequently garnered much media attention. This was the start of a trend for tiny nipped-in waists with full skirts swelling out beneath a small bodice; a trend that eventually trickled down into the wider marketplace.

In the 1980s, Japanese designers brought about a new design aesthetic that stunned the Paris fashion establishment. Rei Kawakubo (of Comme des Garçons) and Yohji Yamamoto broke the mold of power dressing and introduced grunge and deconstruction. By using the color black and adopting less rigid silhouettes, they made a statement against the glamor and excess of power dressing.

Designers such as Dior, Chanel, Rei Kawakubo, and other innovators before and after them, were able to make such revolutionary contributions, not because they were in the right place at the right time, but because they were sensitive to cultural changes and moods, the state of politics, debates on gender, and looking beyond the present.

In the twenty-first century, we are surrounded by a high-tech media culture based around visual and interactive imagery. Magazines and the internet are convenient doorways into the past, present, and future; to different cultures, movements, and personas. These can influence and direct who and what we are, and what we want to be. With all this technology and information readily available, it has become increasingly difficult for a designer to remain competitive and, most importantly, original.

As a designer, to seek something new, to direct a new fad in a bid to stay ahead, authenticity, strong convictions, and market awareness are key.

The zeitgeist

"Zeitgeist" means "the spirit of the times." The role of a designer is not just to design, but to know what fabrics, colors, silhouettes, and proportions will catch the mood or instigate the future. Through the process of research, the designer seeks creative inspiration to stimulate contemporary concepts and experiments, which spark off these design ideas or themes. This is when the designer needs to become the zeitgeist, investigating, hunting, and gathering information to feed his or her imagination—capturing the spirit of the times.

Having a successful grip on the zeitgeist will make you into a rounded, diverse, and individual thinker, and an authority on your design convictions. It will also develop your individual creative integrity and personality. Many students turn to fashion magazines for their source of inspiration. Although this is not wrong—it does make you aware of the industry, the markets, and its movements—magazines should not be used as a primary source for research. The fashion, the photography, and the art direction already exist, so what you have in your hand is someone else's creative final translation. They had a beginning—research that they then developed and translated. You need to find your beginning too.

Primary Research Sources

The following three areas should be considered as the main sources for primary research. These can then be articulated into new trends and design interpretations.

1. **High culture:** fine art, literature, classical music, theater, politics, philosophy, anthropology, sociology, psychology, and arthouse movies.

2. **Popular culture:** television, pop music, movies, and celebrity culture.

3. **Low culture:** street style (street style trends such as hip-hop have become a major influence, translated into fashion trends and disseminated to the masses—this is also known as the "bubble-up" effect), obscure sports or interests, style tribes.

What stimulates me is—LIFE! I think the education imparted to us gives us a culture that is ours, upon which we base ourselves, and from which we take our inspiration. This inspiration evolves along with the evolution of our background.
Martin Margiela

Trends and fashion forecasting

Before the 1960s, the haute couture designers of Paris set hemlines, colors, fabrics, and silhouette trends. Their collections determined the look for the season, which then filtered through into the wider markets. In order to maintain exclusivity, the dissemination of the look was strongly controlled by the haute couture houses and heavily regulated by the Chambre Syndicale in Paris.

Responsible for interpreting and distributing the look, department stores, boutiques, and wholesale companies sent their in-house designers to the couture shows. Large entry fees were paid, and unofficial photography and sketching were strictly forbidden. Unlike today, the fashion press was not allowed to publish any show photographs until several weeks after the event. This was to prevent copies being made before the couture clients received their orders. The entry fee sometimes included a calico toile or paper replica of an haute couture model that could be sold on as a straight copy or adapted to market requirements. Couture houses also had other models that were available for a fee.

This process gave the couture houses and the Chambre Syndicale overall control, secrecy, and exclusivity, and they retained power and influence over the wider fashion

Today, fashion forecasting is big business. It is made up of highly competitive online and consultative agencies predicting the future of fashion in all its aspects, from retail and socioeconomic factors through to trends in color, fabric, print, silhouette, details, and trims.

The forecasters investigate, report, and observe influences that people in the industry do not have time to research. Agencies employ people known as trend chasers or cool hunters, usually with skills gained in the creative industries, sociology, or science. They are sensitive to the cultural atmosphere of the time and are tasked with seeking out, tracking, gathering, and collating information from sources such as style tribes, magazines, flea markets, movies, art, politics, music, social attitudes, environmental issues, science, and technology. Trend tracking also involves looking for changes in demographics (a marketing term for determining the distribution of statistics relating to how people live, behave, their age, gender, income, lifestyle, housing, and social movements).

Martin Raymond, co-founder of leading forecasting agency The Future Laboratory and creative director of *Viewpoint*, the agency's award-winning magazine of trends, brands, futures, and ideas explains: "we have set up a network of around 2,000 contacts that includes people who work in the music industry, academics, people in the club and fashion scenes, and journalists. We use them for what we call 'brailing'—a way of reading the shifts that are set to change a culture."

community. However, in the 1960s and 70s, haute couture lost its supremacy and consequently, the "copying" or "model" system disappeared.

The collapse of the old system left many copiers in limbo, unsure what style was in or what was out. To fill this gap, companies such as IM International in New York, Nigel French in London, and Promostyl in Paris provided a service to inform the industry of the latest trends in color, fabric, and silhouette. This was the beginning of the trend and forecasting industry, which provides information for companies to stay ahead of their competitors and helps them to remain contemporary.

Trend Agencies and their Publications

Agency/Bureau	Type of Publication	Issues
Italex	Trend book	Biannual
Knit Alert	Trend book	Biannual
Milou Ket	Trend book	Biannual
N.O.A.	Trend book	Biannual
Promostyl	Several trend books	Biannual
Sacha Pacha	Several trend books:	Biannual
	Textile View	Quarterly
	View2	Biannual
	View Color	Biannual
	Zoom On Trends	Quarterly
	International Textiles	Quarterly
The Future Laboratory	*Viewpoint* magazine	Biannual
Trendstop	Online subscription	
Trendzine	Online subscription	
Wgsn	Online subscription	
What When & Now	Online subscription	

The data collected by cool hunters is analyzed, broken down, and put together into detailed trend reports with important visual references tracking the future needs and desires of the fashion consumer, either for specific clients or the fashion industry as a whole. The leading agencies produce books, files, or magazines annually, biannually, or quarterly. These publications provide important insights eighteen months to two years ahead of season, and for this reason they are expensive.

The forecasting industry has many good points, but also has a major downside. The distribution of the same seasonal trends to the whole industry can bring about homogeneity within the marketplace.

Individuality becomes redundant because of the lack of different options available. In recent years, designers have become more individual, going against the grain of trends—although inevitably this itself has become a trend. This means it is even more important to have the ability to seek, read, and translate the zeitgeist and express it with individuality in one's own work.

Textile trade exhibitions

Textile trade exhibitions showcase emerging trends in fabric, yarn, and color approximately ten months ahead of season. Their importance is key, as they allow designers, design teams, and manufacturers to experience the raw ingredients directly.

Première Vision, which is held in Paris twice a year, is the largest trade exhibition of its kind. It attracts more than 45,000 visitors over its four days. It spans three vast exhibition halls with more than 800 major exhibitors from Europe and Asia, and specializes in fabrics that cater for every fashion sector from couture to sportswear. In addition, the Indigo section houses leading print studios across Europe exhibiting their latest designs.

Major Textile Exhibitions

Exhibition	Specialism	Market Sector	Date
Première Vision & Indigo Paris, France	Fabrics, prints, & color	All fashion sectors	February & September
Pitti Filati Florence, Italy	Yarns & color	Knitwear	January & July
Moda In. Milan, Italy	Fabrics & color	All fashion sectors	February & September
Tissu Premier Lille, France	Fabrics & color	All fashion sectors	January & September

Fashion stylists

Once upon a time, the fashion stylist was used merely to assist in providing props or accessories for a fashion shoot. The emergence of the fashion stylist as an independent creative identity came about with the advent of new-wave British magazines in the 1980s such as *The Face*, *Dazed and Confused*, and *i-D*. The images on the pages were raw and unadulterated, as opposed to the glossy images of magazines such as *Vogue*.

Stylists Katie Grand and Katy England have played major roles in determining the direction of major fashion brands and magazines, which in turn have influenced fashion trends. Katie Grand began her career at *Dazed and Confused* and became fashion director of *The Face*, where she applied her edgy skills. She explains; "lots of stylists work from the clothes and then have an idea about the shoot, whereas I think of a reference—photography, art…" Katie is currently editor-in-chief of *PoP*, and acts as a consultant for the likes of Prada, Miu Miu, and Louis Vuitton.

Katy England established herself as an innovative fashion image-maker at *Dazed and Confused* and as fashion editor at *Another Magazine*. Admiring her style and personal aesthetic, Alexander McQueen made her creative director of his label and made sure she was heavily involved at every stage of the process, from research through to catwalk shows. She has also worked with Topshop as a creative consultant for the Kate Moss collection.

Melanie Ward is another innovative stylist who has applied her evocative cool style to *i-D* magazine and to numerous designers and brands including Helmut Lang, Jil Sander, Calvin Klein, Yohji Yamamoto, and Levi's. As editor of the US edition of *Harper's Bazaar* since 1995, she has brought about some of the most innovative imagery and styling found in mainstream publications.

Away from magazines, celebrity stylist Patricia Field is best known for styling the main characters in the hugely popular TV series *Sex and the City*. Her work on the show helped to launch trends for handbags, sunglasses, shoes, and also the celebrity fashion persona, which millions of fashion consumers have bought into.

Before the advent of the stylist, it was the designer who was solely responsible for making style decisions. Today, designers have less time because they are involved with designing several lines as opposed to just one. Together with the increased pressure for new and innovative presentations in magazines and on the catwalk, responsibility has shifted toward the stylist, who is now an integral part of the overall fashion presentation.

Fashion editors

The power of fashion editors cannot be ignored. They continue to play a major role in highlighting or setting off a fashion moment. Although editors are not the primary source of a trend, their coverage of fashion shows and their creation of fashion stories bring key looks to the wider public, which then buys into the trends.

Carmel Snow, the legendary fashion editor of *Harper's Bazaar* US, labeled Christian Dior's collection in 1947 as the "New Look" and gave the collection ample coverage. This endorsement not only increased Dior's status as a designer but also publicized his silhouette and look, which others simulated.

Anna Wintour, editor of American *Vogue*, is acclaimed as having foreseen the merger of celebrity and fashion back in the early 1990s—a trend that is still prevalent today. She often runs issues with a celebrity on the front cover, thereby making an endorsement and setting a trend.

Anna Wintour
Anna Wintour, the infamous fashion editor of American *Vogue*, is one of the most influential people in fashion today. Her ability to foresee special fashion moments has given her the authority to set trends and endorse and promote young designers who will be stars of the future.

The Fashion Calendar

Predominantly based around the seasonal changes of the year, the annual fashion calendar is action-packed and relentless. The fashion industry works toward two key delivery dates: spring/summer (end of January/early February), and fall/winter (end of July/early August). Each delivery point depends on a cycle of events that starts with concept and ends with distribution. Companies from every market level, as well as integral sectors such as forecasters, manufacturers, and retailers, must be well organized and intelligently structured in order to cope with the fashion calendar. Similarly, organizations that put on trade shows and fashion weeks, such as the British Fashion Council, Première Vision, and IMG, work together to ensure there are no overlaps or clashes between events.

Reproduced here is a typical yearly schedule for a ready-to-wear label, outlining the order of key events that take place throughout the year.

January

- Milan Fashion Week menswear fall/winter collections

- Paris Fashion Week menswear fall/winter collections

- Paris haute couture shows spring/summer collections

- Pitti Filati Yarn and color spring/summer (for next year)

- Tissu Premier Fabrics and color spring/summer (for next year)

- Deliveries for this year's spring/summer menswear and womenswear collections

February

- Première Vision & Indigo fabrics, color, and print spring/summer (for next year)

- New York Fashion Week womenswear and menswear fall/winter collections

- London Fashion Week womenswear and menswear (MAN) fall/winter collections

- Milan Fashion Week womenswear fall/winter collections

- Paris Fashion Week womenswear (prêt-a- porter) fall/winter collections

- Selling at trade shows, showrooms, agents

March

- End of Paris Fashion Week womenswear (prêt-a- porter) fall/winter collections

- Selling at trade shows, showrooms, agents

April

- Order book closed for fall/winter collections
- preparations made for production

May

- Sampling for spring/summer collections (for next year)

June

- Sampling for spring/summer collections (for next year)

- Milan Fashion Week menswear spring summer collections (for next year)

- Paris Fashion Week menswear spring/summer collections (for next year)

July

- End of Paris Fashion Week menswear spring/summer collections (for next year)

- **Pitti Filati** yarn and color fall/winter (for next year)

- **Paris haute couture shows** fall/winter collections

August

- Samples for spring/summer (for next year), final adjustment in time for shows and selling

- Deliveries for this year's fall/winter collections

September

- Première Vision & Indigo fabrics, color, and print fall/winter (for next year)

- New York Fashion Week womenswear and menswear spring/summer collections

- London Fashion Week womenswear and menswear (MAN) spring/summer collections

- Milan Fashion Week womenswear spring/summer collections

- Paris Fashion Week womenswear (prêt-a- porter) spring/summer collections

- Selling at trade shows, showrooms, agents

October

- End of Paris Fashion Week

- womenswear (prêt-a- porter) spring/summer collections

- Selling at trade shows, showrooms, agents

- Order books closed for spring/summer collections and preparations made for production

November

- Sampling for fall/winter collections (for next year)

December

- Sampling for fall/winter collections (for next year)

The fashion cycle

The fashion cycle is a sequential chain of events that demonstrates the process from concept to delivery per season. Each event has its own particular job, importance, and position within the cycle that makes the process function efficiently.

Contrary to popular belief, the role of a designer is not solely based around innovation and creativity. This diagram helps to identify and define the various roles a designer must embrace in order for the final product to be successful. Therefore, alongside the role of visionary and lead creative, a designer needs to have 3D technical understanding, manufacturing techniques, communication skills, administration skills, management skills, an understanding of the production methods, and overall market awareness—knowing what the customer wants, analyzing successes and failures, and implementing changes for the next cycle.

FASHION CYCLE

1. Forecasting

Color trends
Style trends
Trend stories

2. Trade fairs

Fabric and color: Première Vision, Moda In.
Yarn and color: Pitti Filati
Order fabric and color swatches, hangers, and price lists. These provide important reference in the design stage

3. Design

Research and inspiration
Design development
Design and develop selling collection or pre-collection/range-building
Design runway collection and showpiece outfits
Design seasonal drops: cruise/Christmas collections
Fabric and color decisions

4. 3D product developments

Toiling
Silhouette pattern development
Finishings and trims
Fittings on model
Final fabric decisions, order sample lengths

5. First samples

Garments cut and made in final fabric
Final fittings: changes made if needed (the behavior of certain fabrics can vary the cut of the garment, therefore necessary alterations to design or fabrics at this stage can save time and money)

6. Fashion week and selling

Selling/runway collection and showpieces ready for Fashion Week and selling
Orders taken from buyers: New York, London, Milan, and Paris Fashion Weeks

all have static selling trade shows.
A hired showroom space,
selling agent's showroom, or the
company's own showroom is
preferred as a selling amphitheater
The order book will give the company
a heads up in regards to the next
fashion cycle—what they can and
can't afford to produce

7. Production

Make an assessment of the orders
Order fabrics for production run
Complete production patterns and
pattern grading for sizing
Manufacture the orders and check
quality. Manufacturing options are:
in-house, cottage industry, CMT (cut,
make, trim), or full package
manufacturers. Chain stores use
overseas production plants that have
specialist machinery to deal with
high-volume production runs.
Packaging: swing tickets, etc

8. Shipment and delivery

Company's own retail outlets,
boutiques, stores
Seasonal drops
Online boutiques

9. Retail sales

Consumer interests and sales analysis

10. Start of next cycle

Sales history gives an indication of what
key looks and silhouettes can be taken
forward with minor modifications into
the next cycle

The production calendar

The production calendar lays down a practical framework of consecutive procedures to be carried out in order to deliver spring/summer and fall/winter collections on time.

As the calendar demonstrates, the production, research, and design processes for the two seasons cross over at certain points. The framework helps to monitor any possible glitches that might affect deliveries—for example, orders not being finished on time due

to buttons being the wrong size. Effective and efficient management is crucial for all fashion market levels—more so for the smaller independent labels, as they need to juggle between seasons effectively in order to stay afloat. This continuous design and production process is an economical and cashflow-efficient way of working as long as production, deliveries, and payments remain on schedule.

Lead times are an important factor in determining the amount of time it takes for a collection to be completed, from concept to retail. For mass-market retailers, short lead times are vital to ensure continuous quick mid-seasonal drops. Production management has to be carefully considered in order to meet the schedules that short lead times impose. Most mass-market retailers have offshore production facilities, mainly in Asia for its obvious advantage of being cheaper. However, this can also lengthen the lead time because of the long distances involved, possible delays in communication, and the scattered nature of the production. Unlike its competitors, the Spanish retailer Zara keeps its design team, production, and distribution centers all together in Spain. This strategy has proven to be successful: the brand has short lead times between collection drops; problems can be fixed physically on site rather than by email or fax, and problems with communication are nil.

Sophie Wightman
Illustration by designer Sophie Wightman. She creates a mood for her spring/summer collection that suggests a young, sassy, and playful print-oriented collection directed at a specific market.

Spring/Summer	
March	Research fabrics and design development
April	Final decisions made for fabrics and colors Silhouette and pattern development
May	Finalize patterns and start sampling
June	Continue sampling and finish any loose ends
July	Finish sampling and final fittings
August	Selling period begins Prepare for Fashion Week
September	Collections presented at Fashion Week Selling continues
October	Order books closed for the season Analysis of orders ready for production
November	Materials and trims ordered for production Production begins
December	Monitor production
January	Monitor production Production begins to arrive
February	First deliveries to stores Production continues to arrive Continue deliveries
March	Final deliveries End of season

Fall/Winter	
September	Research fabrics and design development
October	Final decisions made for fabrics and colors Silhouette and pattern development
November	Finalize patterns and start sampling
December	Continue sampling and finish any loose ends
January	Finish sampling and final fittings
February	Selling period begins Prepare for Fashion Week
March	Collections presented at Fashion Week Selling continues
April	Order books closed for the season Analysis of orders ready for production
May	Materials and trims ordered for production Production begins
June	Monitor production
July	Monitor production Production begins to arrive
August	First deliveries to stores Production continues to arrive Continue deliveries
September	Final deliveries End of season

Collections and ranges

Spring/summer and fall/winter are the two most important collection drops of the year, and for most independent and small labels this still remains the case. However, in a bid to boost sales and market share, the large established designer brands such as Chanel and Ralph Lauren have additional seasonal drops alongside their mainline collections that are primarily designed for a particular time of the year. "Cruise" or "resort" collections are aimed at the summer holiday period, whereas Christmas collections are led by the festive season and mainly includes party outfits such as "the little black dress" in a variety of styles.

The big chain retailers employ the "fast fashion" model, which enables them to drop new collections and colorways at varied times within a given season. In essence, these mid-seasonal drops are derivatives of the main collection. Clever marketing and branding initiatives such as applying specific names and stories to the collections give the clothes independence and originality. This offers the consumer more choice and variety compared to the singular drop per season made by most independent and ready-to-wear labels.

However, to remain competitive and ensure economic survival, smaller designer labels have responded to the fast fashion model by launching pre-collections between one and three months ahead of their main runway presentations. Unlike the runway collections, which are geared toward pleasing the press and driving up notability, the pre-collection is seen as an important selling tool, giving buyers an opportunity to view the collection's primary mood and key looks, and place early orders.

The role of fashion weeks

Primarily a marketing event, fashion weeks are an important part of the fashion calendar. Each show can incite and maintain an aura of exclusivity. They are an opportunity for designers and their collections to get noticed and be endorsed by influential fashion editors. The week-long event serves the industry by promoting and stimulating national and international interest from buyers and press, as well as supporting the city's local trade and boosting the commercial community at large, such as hotels, restaurants, bars, and fashion retailers.

The couture and ready-to-wear shows of the early to mid-twentieth century were primarily set up as a promotional and selling tool for the designers and design houses situated in Paris. The Chambre Syndicale insisted that its members design and showcase seasonal collections twice a year: spring/summer in January and fall/winter in July. This key regulation still exists today, and is imitated by the ready-to-wear designers, albeit at different times of the year (in order to avoid any logistical clashes and to maximize press coverage and attendance for both events).

The collapse of the traditional haute couture industry and the establishment of a new fashion hierarchy helped to form the competitive landscape of biannual fashion weeks as we know them today. To be crowned "fashion capital of the world" by the press brings with it financial rewards for the designers, the city's fashion industry, and the country at large. The big four fashion cities are New York, London, Milan, and Paris. Each has a specific persona built around its cultural heritage and characteristics, which in turn have a significant influence on its designers' approach to fashion. Designers who specifically wish to be aligned with a city's particular qualities usually have working studios in that city or regularly show as part of the city's fashion week.

Fashion weeks provide opportunities for new talents to emerge and get noticed. In addition, the collaborative inventions between stylists, hair and make-up artists, show producers, and designers may generate extensive press coverage and help to trigger seasonal trends.

Although the international buyers and press remain loyal to the big four fashion capitals, new cities such as Sao Paulo, Tokyo, Shanghai, Sydney, and Mumbai have begun to emerge as fashion capitals in their own right. Their infrastructure is not yet as strong as their more established counterparts, and therefore commercial success and worldwide recognition is so far limited, but that may all change in coming years.

Overleaf: Fashion Weeks
Left to right: London, New York, Milan, and Paris Fashion Weeks.

London Fashion Week is known for promoting young, spirited, avant-garde designers, who push the boundaries of fashion. With little regard for commercial success, concept and theatrical presentations take center stage. The likes of Galliano, McQueen, Chalayan, and Westwood have been products of the London fashion scene.

Dominated by Italian designers, Milan Fashion Week has a reputation for presenting a sultry and sexy grown-up style. Dolce & Gabbana typify the Milanese look; here they present their spring/summer 2010 ready-to-wear collection.

Regarded as the epicenter of world fashion, Paris is historically characterized by its luxurious haute couture industry and sophisticated ready-to-wear aesthetic. However, recently, younger and more edgy designers such as Martine Sitbon and the Japanese avant-garde have brought a contemporary element to Paris Fashion Week. Here, remaining true to the Parisian ideal, designer Andrew Gn presents his spring/summer 2010 ready-to-wear collection.

American designer Donna Karan presents her spring/ summer 2010 collection at New York Fashion Week. Of the "big four" fashion capitals, New York is the most commercially oriented. Made up of mostly American designers together with some international labels from Europe, the emphasis is on wearable fashion.

From Sketch to Dress: the Design Process

It's great to tell a story in a collection, but you must never forget that, despite all the fantasy, the thing is about clothes. And all the time while you are editing to make the impact stronger, you have to remember that, at the end of the day, there has to be a collection and it has to be sold.

John Galliano

Amid all the creativity and razzmatazz, it should never be forgotten that the fashion industry is a commercial operation. Season after season, fashion designers need to provide something new to entice buyers and to excite the fashion press. As a designer, whether you work independently or as part of a design team, you must be able to initiate new ideas, moods, and themes, and direct both the creative and the commercial path for a collection.

This chapter explores the complete process of design from the initial stages of research and development through to the final product. It introduces the fundamental aspects concerned with two-dimensional and three-dimensional design that enables a sketch to come to fruition and be fully realized into a tangible product.

Who are you designing for?

The starting point of any design brief is that you, the designer, know and understand what market level and customer you are designing for: haute couture, ready-to-wear, or mass market? Once this is decided, you can start to establish what types of designs, quality of fabrics, colors, details, and production methods are relevant to that market level. This is vital: blindly designing for a market without prior knowledge of the customer, price, or expected quality will be a costly mistake on all fronts.

Far left: Hanna Buswell
This knitwear designer presents her 2009 fall/winter collection. The wearable shapes, together with a play on color, geometric shapes, and stripes gives the collection a contemporary edge.

Left: Amus Leung
Amus Leung presents her 2009 fall/winter collection. This fake fur black dress has an exaggerated modern silhouette aimed at the ready-to-wear market.

Opposite: Jess Holmes
A page from Jess Holmes' sketchbook contains collaged elements from children's memorabilia, demonstrating the designer's initial thoughts for a collection.

Conduct some market research in order to understand who your competitors are and what they offer in terms of design aesthetic, quality, branding, variations within the range, and price point. Speak to sales staff; find out what items sell the most; what sort of customers buy the stock—are they young, wealthy, or a mixture?

Quality of cut, fabric, and fit can never really be appreciated on hangers, so don't be afraid to try on your competitors' clothes. This will give you a better understanding of the garment; how the fabric, cut, details, proportions, and silhouette work together in unison. Understand what works well, and question what doesn't.

It doesn't matter what market level you are designing for, you should still be knowledgeable of all market sectors and aware of their product ranges. Keeping yourself well informed will help to establish and strengthen your own position within the fashion market.

Research and investigation

Design ideas do not appear like magic; there has to be investigation, visual stimulation, creative dialogue, questioning, understanding, and analysis. This gives the work depth and contemporary relevance. The process of research and investigation is an exciting time for a designer, looking into new sources of inspiration, feeding the imagination, and educating the creative mind. It also provides respite from the stresses of the business side of fashion.

There are two branches to fashion design research. The first is to gather together actual, tangible objects to inspire ideas

for texture and handle. This might involve collecting fabrics, buttons, zippers, textiles, found objects such as shells, granny's old jewelry box, or retro bric-à-brac. You can make drawings and take photographs to use as reference material later. In the case of fabrics, small swatches provide an initial reference for quality, handle, and price. Similarly, fastenings and trims can be bought in small quantities to provide an important reminder during the design stage.

The second method of research is slightly more removed; it is more visual and investigative than tangible. Books, magazines, design journals, and the internet provide information and images that you might not be able to experience directly; for example, an interesting building on the other side of the world, or documents concerning historical movements. These sources can offer detailed background, philosophy, and imagery, which can be photocopied or downloaded to trigger creative thought.

Fashion is not something that exists in dresses only. Fashion is in the sky, in the street, fashion has to do with ideas, the way we live, what is happening.

Coco Chanel

You should explore both types of research to help you improve both theoretical knowledge and practical skills such as drawing and the application of color. Information gathering, recording, and decision-making are important organizational and reflective skills that are necessary in becoming an all-round creative practitioner.

Research sources

The essence of research is to look for clues that will educate and inspire you, and lead you into further investigation of the unknown, with the aim of creating fresh ideas. As an aspiring designer, an understanding of contextual and historical fashion is important. It can become a continuous source of inspiration and make you question the past and present in order to evaluate the future.

So, along with information from historical costume and fashion, where will these clues come from? Typical starting points include flea markets, second-hand shops, *National Geographic* journals, museums, libraries, the natural world, new technologies, and street and youth cultures. Or they could come from essays, such as "Black Moods" by Gabriel Ramin Schor, or "The End of Perspective?" by Vincent Pécoil. They could come via the new

generation of collectors and taxidermists who are making taxidermy hip again. Maybe it's a book you have read or been meaning to read; George Orwell's classic *Down and Out in Paris and London*, or a modern classic such as *A Clockwork Orange* by Anthony Burgess. The clue could be in the lyrics or music of Jimi Hendrix, Bob Dylan, Chopin, or Duran Duran, or maybe a collaboration of all four. Art movements, classical art, contemporary art, sculpture, and exhibitions could hold vital clues. A film by Francis Ford Coppola may be littered with clues. A provocative photograph by Rankin or the sensual and sweeping forms created by the architect Santiago Calatrava may inspire a creative reaction. Or you could take a quote from the old master himself, Christian Dior: "it was while I was with Robert Piguet that I learned how to 'omit' … Piguet knew that elegance can be found only in simplicity."

Many designers constantly revisit the past as a source of inspiration and influence. This may be in the form of fine art and literature as well as historical dress. Rather than merely recycling the original work, their glamorous and sometimes mischievous designs are personal interpretations and not literal reproductions. Wherever you get inspiration, make sure the subject matter is of interest to you, relevant to the brief, and fully investigated and understood. Superficial research will lead to work that lacks depth and consideration.

The muse

A muse is a person or character who is a source of inspiration; someone who can set the tone for a collection or instigate the house look through their personality and unique individual style. This could be a character from a book or film, an influential personality from the past or present, or a celebrity—as Audrey Hepburn was for Givenchy. A muse could be a fantasy character, or a photograph or portrait of someone who represents a certain attitude. Any of these starting points could help establish a theme for the next creative direction.

This character becomes the central figurehead for all creative discussion; for example, what colors would she wear? Does she wear pants? If so, are they high-waisted, cropped, or flared? Asking questions relating to the muse will help to identify and capture the spirit of the collection.

Collating research

Once your information has been gathered, you need to pull it together, making connections via unusual but interesting and stimulating compositions that will lead to a design direction. Collating this information in a sketchbook, daily journal, or on a blank wall will help you to digest, understand, and pursue a line of enquiry. Sketchbooks are not just about

displaying found imagery or objects; the purpose is to add a new personal twist, a new taste, a new spin, to juxtapose subjects that are modern, market-relevant, and unexpected. Care must be taken not to reuse the literal flavor from original resources, otherwise innovation will play little or no part within the process.

Collages, drawings, colors, fabrics, and descriptive words or sentences can all help to give meaning and depth to imagery. Further reflection, analysis, questioning,

Emily Robus
Designer Emily Robus sketches and collages together an image of her muse, depicting the character of her fantasy woman to inspire her collection.

and cross-referencing between pages will eventually lead to a conclusion. Beware that an overedited sketchbook will translate into stagnant and uninspiring pages. Remain enthusiastic and courageous throughout the process and this will lead the way for an exciting, raw, and personal outcome.

Over time and with experience, you will eventually develop your own individual approach to research. The process of investigating and collating information will become second nature. However, sketchbooks should display an original approach with a contemporary outlook. The emphasis should remain on experimentation, refining current skills, and attaining deeper knowledge and understanding in order to find inspiration and present a design proposition that is fully resolved and market-relevant.

Mood boards or storyboards offer a quick and useful way to assemble information and present a focused idea to a client or panel. In essence, they are edited translations of the research that has been collated in sketchbooks. They demonstrate a logical journey that clearly emphasizes the look, color, fabric, and overall theme for a collection. Depending upon the collection, key words such as "dark," "masculine," or "moody" can be used to highlight the mood for a collection. Occasionally, according to the client or company you are presenting to, information such as customer, mood, color, and fabric can be presented on separate boards. This will help you present the collection in a coherent way.

Left and below:
Calum Harvey
Menswear designer Calum Harvey's sketchbook demonstrates his thought processes, from the original sketch, then to initial draping on the stand, and finally to realizing the first 3D prototype.

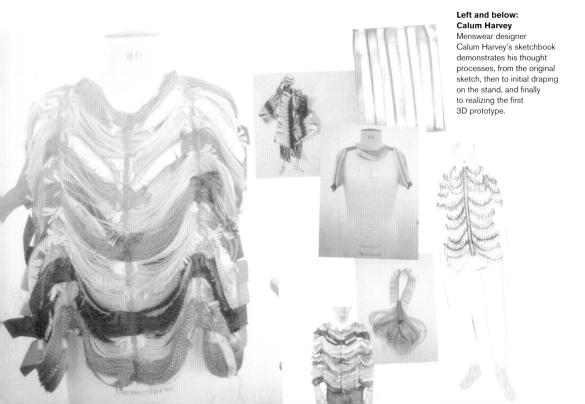

The importance of drawing

Drawing is a vital skill; it is a tool that helps you to record data and to communicate and develop your ideas. As you explore the research further, drawing helps you decipher information and make sense of the research, providing focused information and inspiration that can be carried into design development. Drawing allows a designer to communicate ideas and information. The process trains the eye to see design details, texture, and proportion within garments and in relation to the figure. In industry, being able to render quick sketches can immediately communicate an idea to the design team, and provide impetus for a direction. Sketches can also solve problems, thereby saving time and money.

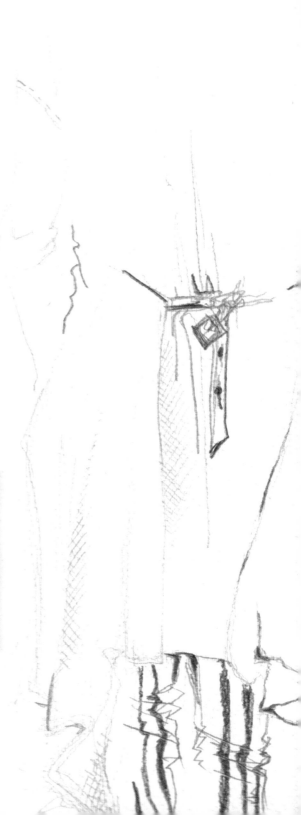

Above and right:
Marie Pranning
Menswear designer Marie Pranning plays with different intensities of line and the application of block color to create depth and investigate positive and negative space in her sketches. This enables the designer to explore and finesse the right direction for her collection.

When a design is so overwhelming as to be paralyzing, don't wait for clarity to arrive before beginning to draw. Drawing is not simply a way of depicting a design solution; it is itself a way of learning about the problem you are trying to solve.

Matthew Frederick (from *101 Things I Learned in Architecture School*)

Exploring different media such as pencil, charcoal, paints, or pen and ink adds new dimensions to drawings, giving the research new visual aspects such as quality of line, texture, and tonality. As your mark-making becomes more experimental, you will discover new techniques and develop a personal visual language.

Not everyone is good at drawing, and it can be a daunting and intimidating task. Maintaining a relaxed approach to drawing will help you create fluid lines that may inspire the shape of a silhouette, drape, or an unusual cut. Always remember that your sketchbook is a place in which to discover new ideas and to jot down quick thoughts and possibilities—it is not about perfection at this point.

The silhouette

The silhouette is important in defining the outline of the body shape produced by a garment or an outfit. The silhouette can have a great impact on the catwalk and leave a lasting impression. The overall shape and structure is often the first big moment, followed by the details, fabrics, and trims. The silhouette is key to the success of any outfit or collection. It can help to present the current scene, or establish an attitude and overall look for a collection.

Right: Arsida Smajili
Arsida Smajli uses wood veneer to create a modern conceptual fashion silhouette.

As views on femininity, sexuality, gender, politics, and lifestyles have changed, designers have created body shapes to express the attitude of the times and to rebel against accepted norms. The twentieth century saw many versions of the silhouette evolve, ranging from the accentuated, nipped-in waists and padded hips of the early 1900s, to the "flapper" look of the 1920s, the New Look created by Dior in 1947, the power dressing of the 1980s, and the figure-hugging dresses of the 1990s.

While in the past, each decade could be said to have its own look, the 2000s saw many different silhouettes, from deconstructed to tailored depending upon the designer and label. Designers often have their own trademark, individual silhouettes. Martin Margiela has a distinct take on deconstructed beauty, while Jil Sander offers a modern tailored silhouette, combining both traditional and modern elements of construction and finishing. Sophia Kokosalaki's work is easily identifiable by her Grecian silhouette and her modern interpretation of classicized draping.

As part of your initial research and design development in sketchbooks, key adjectives such as soft, cropped, stark, severe, or voluminous can be aligned with the drawn shapes, helping you to further explore and define the desired silhouette. These experimental combinations of imagery, drawings, and verbal descriptions, together with stand work, can begin to be translated into first drafts of a personalized silhouette.

Above left:
Emma Mulcair
Emma Mulcair uses silk and neoprene fabrics to create a modern version of Dior's classic hourglass silhouette.

Above right:
Sian Lendrum
Sian Lendrum plays with layering, color, and transparency to create two silhouettes within one design.

Proportion, line, and balance

Within a silhouette, proportion and line play important roles in bringing together a balanced and harmonious outfit that is pleasing to the eye and flatters the body.

Proportion refers to the application of the size of separate components relating to the whole. In fashion terms, the human body is the whole, while the shoulders, neck, arms, legs, torso, hips, waist, and so on, make up the separate components that can divide the body into vertical, horizontal, diagonal, or curved lines. Blocks of color, fabric, texture, or print can also divide the body and create proportional zones. Good proportion can be defined as the harmonious relationship between different lines and sizes judged against the body—the whole.

Intelligent and quirky proportions can be achieved by playing with length, width, and volume. For example, raising the waistline of trousers above the natural waist creates the appearance of elongating the legs and shortening the body. Alexander McQueen's infamous "bumster" pants did the opposite; by dropping the waistline well below the natural waist, his pants gave the illusion of an accentuated torso and shorter legs.

Silhouette and line are closely related and highlight the nature of the cut for a garment. However, the physical lines created by seams, darts, textile patterns, or sweeping drapes distinguish line from silhouette. A line can lead the viewer to look across, up, down, or around the body, creating illusions of narrowness or fullness.

As a general rule, vertical and straight lines lengthen the body and give a structured or masculine look. Horizontal lines give the illusion of width and tend to shorten the body. Curved lines are generally more sympathetic to the female form. They create softer feminine contours that minimize the waist and accentuate the bust and hips. Bias-cut garments produce a diagonal line across and around the body that gives a flowing and figure-hugging curvaceous look.

Balance is the overarching factor that is needed to bring together the different aspects of a garment. Harmonious balance can be achieved by applying equal strength or importance to the design elements, including proportion, line, and color.

If the body is vertically divided through the middle, you will find that each half is symmetrical. Our brains are hardwired to seek symmetry, and this sense of symmetrical balance is often carried through into clothing design. This is created by identical and aligned details mirrored from left to right, such as pockets, collars, lapels, cuffs, sleeves, darts, and seams.

Opposite left and center: Kate Williams
In the first image, Kate Williams creates perfect balance by using three colors distributed proportionally in an innovative way. In the second image, she achieves balance through block color, lasercut layering, and clever weight distribution to create harmony between two extreme front jacket lengths.

Opposite right: Calum Harvey
Menswear designer Calum Harvey plays with extreme proportions around the neck and shoulders to create a modern vision for his menswear, yet he retains the essence of a wearable and acceptable men's silhouette.

Horizontal balance is concerned with the relationship between top and bottom. The natural dividing line between the top and bottom half of the body is at the waist. However, unlike vertical balance, these two parts are unequal—the top half is shorter and the bottom half is longer. This is an obstacle that needs to be overcome in design, as it is easy to create top-heavy or bottom-heavy outfits. A top-heavy outfit might have the design focused around the shoulders, neck, or torso, whereas bottom-heavy designs can make the bottom half appear large and shapeless.

Asymmetric balance is seen in disproportional or deconstructed garments that have been counterbalanced by small or big design features in one or several carefully considered areas that act as an "echo" or "weight", providing an overall balanced shape. This has been a key feature in the work of Japanese and Belgian designers such as Yohji Yamamoto and Martin Margiela, who question and manipulate the principles of balance to express an avant-garde design aesthetic.

Breaking the rules can bring a unique quality to the design, as long as there remains a sense of balance and sensitivity in regards to the body.

Proportion, line, and balance offer many design possibilities that can drastically improve a design, but can also spoil it. Something as simple as playing with the size of buttons or pockets, or something more complex such as moving seams, can have a pleasing and striking effect or, on the other hand, a negative impact on the overall outcome. Drawing and stand work will help train your eye and give you a deeper appreciation of these factors.

Color and fabric

Color and fabric are central to design research and to the design process. Both are key ingredients without which fashion cannot exist. Using these elements imaginatively and with sensitive handling in relation to the silhouette will enable you to successfully create the total look. On the other hand, mishandling color and fabric, or designing incorrect proportions, will leave you with detrimental results.

Color is an integral part of all our lives; everything we see and interact with is in color. Not only does color give us an objective view about the world, it affects how we feel. Research carried out by psychologists provides evidence on how people respond to color; for example, blues and greens have been shown to lower blood pressure and have a calming influence, while red can speed up the heart rate and have an energizing effect.

Certain colors have preconceived connotations that have evolved from various cultural and social symbolisms. For example, pink is associated with sweetness, gray is seen as businesslike, beige is considered neutral and safe.

Your research will provide the initial inspiration for a color palette. Certain colors will take prominence, thereby capturing the mood of the collection. By trying different

Below left:
Hannah Taylor
Knitwear designer Hannah Taylor uses a clash of bright colors and oversized silhouettes to present a lively and humorous 2009 fall/winter menswear collection.

Below center: Laura Yiannakou
Designer Laura Yiannakou's sophisticated use of color and stripes enables her to present a young, sassy ready-to-wear collection.

Below right: Emile Claiborne
Designer Emile Claiborne creates a modern and glamorous sexy rock chick look by using contemporary silhouettes and proportions together with innovative textiles. This outfit features different tones of blue, ranging from bright electric blue to deep navy verging on black.

combinations of color and applying contrast, highlight, block, or tonal colors to the main color group, a final palette can be formulated. Whatever method is used, proportional distribution of color is crucial.

Resources for color inspiration include trend agencies and fabric fairs. Both publish dedicated "color" magazines and hold seminars and presentations that inform the fashion industry of the latest color trends and new technological breakthroughs, such as eco-friendly dyes. Designers sometimes become known for using certain trademark colors and palettes; for example, Valentino is known for his use of red, while Ann Demeulemeester is recognized for her use of black and dark palettes. As a designer, you might form personal preferences for certain colors, or use color to manipulate a certain emotional response from your customers.

Below: Hannah Taylor
Hannah Taylor's sketchbook shows her playing with colored yarn to configure the right color palette for one of her designs. This exercise helps to achieve the right balance and proportion of color for the design.

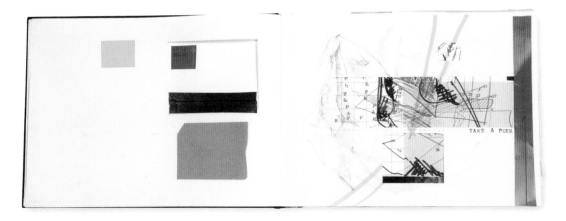

Useful Color Terminology

Primary colors: Red, yellow, and blue.

Secondary colors: Orange, green, and purple. These colors are created by mixing two primary colors together. For example, mixing yellow and red together makes orange.

Tertiary colors: These colors are created by mixing together a primary color and a secondary color. There are many combinations of tertiary colors depending upon how they are mixed; for example, yellow and orange; red and orange; red and purple; blue and purple; blue and green; and yellow and green.

Warm colors: Colors associated with the sun and fire, such as yellow, red, and orange.

Cool colors: Colors associated with grass and the sea, such as green and blue.

Pastel: A color tinted with white; for example, red mixed with white makes pink.

Monochrome: One color or shades of one color.

Tonal colors: For example, if red is the single base color, it would have different degrees of intensities to form a family of various shades of red.

Neutrals: Beige, gray, brown, khaki.

Earth colors: Colors associated with nature and earth, such as brown, green, gray, and yellow.

Contrasts: Colors that are completely different from each other, more than likely opposites on the color wheel; for example, blue and orange.

Accent color: A color used in small quantities, but that has strong visual impact.

Opposite: Hayley Crompton
This print designer uses a simple, modern silhouette as a canvas for an intricate black-and-white print. Hints of highlight colors together with primary yellow make a strong statement.

Far left: Ruth Green
This knitwear designer exploits the stretchy nature of knitted fabric to create a body-hugging outfit. Horizontal lines and block color are used innovatively to create a perfectly balanced and proportioned outfit.

Left: Marie Pranning
This menswear designer uses a palette of off-whites in lightweight wools and silks to create a modern and casual interpretation of a tailored suit.

Knowledge of different fabrics and understanding how to apply various qualities of fabrics to your designs is a fundamental skill. Fabrics have their own aesthetic personalities, which can provide inspiration through the way they look, feel, and handle.

For some designers, fabric is the first point of research and dictates the theme or sets the mood for the collection. Other designers decipher the research first and along the journey interpret the information into fabric and color stories.

I'm fascinated by fabric, the way it can be architectural.
Ally Capellino

There is a huge array of fabrics available. They have different finishes, weights, textures, and properties that are specific to certain garment designs, market sectors, and seasons. Fabrics need to be appropriate for the purpose of a garment. For example, Gore-Tex fabric is specially designed for water resistance and for keeping the body cool through its breathable structure; it is therefore ideal for sportswear and outerwear.

As a rule, heavier-weight fabrics tend to be used for fall/winter garments and lighter weights for spring/summer. For example, woollen fabrics are traditionally used for fall/winter, although there are varieties of lightweight wools and wool mixes that have been developed specifically for spring/summer collections. Denim, cotton, silk, satin, and jersey fabrics tend to be used all year round; some specialist fabric mills offer seasonal variations that give the fabrics an updated and contemporary look.

As a designer, you must have reasonable expectations as to how a fabric will behave. The weight and handle of a fabric can determine not only the way the garment falls but more importantly how it works with the silhouette. Not all fabrics can be applied or forced into a design that is not compatible with its characteristics. For example, chiffon, which is very feminine, soft, floaty, lightweight, and see-through, will not be a suitable fabric for a functional coat, whereas wool or Teflon-coated cotton would fit the purpose.

As a designer, you will have the creative freedom to put together combinations of fabrics and colors within a collection or garment. Not everyone has a natural aptitude for color and fabric. Knowing what works and what doesn't comes with practice, exploring the possibilities, and continuous self-critical reflection. Keeping yourself informed is important; go to fabric fairs and color presentations to build up your knowledge base and awareness.

I look at the role of the body in different cultural contexts, such as architecture, science, or nature, and see how these approaches can be applied to clothing.
Hussein Chalayan

Design development

According to the brief, the market level, and the season, your research pages will have explored various lines of enquiry as well as the fundamentals—silhouette, line, proportion, balance, details, function, color, and fabric. By analyzing this information and editing the many drawings, sketches, and collages you have produced, some clear design ideas and features will have emerged, along with the overall theme and mood. At this point, you should give the collection a working title; it will keep you focused. Now all your information needs to be developed further.

Essentially, design development is a way of refining and fully exploring all the design possibilities. Rendering continuous drawings and playing with details, proportions, color, fabric, and outfit combinations will build a comprehensive body of work.

Usually, to create one design, up to a hundred different variations will be drawn until the design has been fully exhausted and the designer is satisfied. For example, when considering the final design for a jacket, once the silhouette has been established, the length and width of the sleeves and hem, the center opening, lapel and collar size, pockets, seams, details, and darts will all be explored intensely with subtle variations to achieve the end result, demonstrating line, proportion, and balance within the silhouette. The jacket must also be judged against other garments that will make up a complete outfit. Further drawings will need to be rendered, including adjusting color and fabrics to refine the total look.

Above: Leila McGlew
A page from this designer's sketchbook shows how she has used a personal approach to develop her designs. By applying color and folded paper, she collages her graphic shapes onto a photocopied template.

Left: Natalie Bennett
This designer sketches and collages photographs of draped stand work together to help develop and finalize her designs.

Putting together a collection and range

At the outset, the design brief will have set out the size of the collection, market level, key garments such as dresses, tailored jackets, pants, skirts, and shirts, and certain customer preferences; for example, sales analysis from previous seasons may show how some colors or designs have sold better than others. These considerations will all be key parts of designing the collection.

The number of outfits a collection contains will depend on the size of the company. Due to restraints on finance and resources, small independent ready-to-wear labels may produce fifteen to thirty outfits (or twenty to eighty individual pieces) per season. By contrast, the likes of Prada, Calvin Klein, and Givenchy have the infrastructure to generate up to eighty outfits every season. Final-year fashion graduates are expected to design and produce a collection of somewhere between six and eight outfits, fully realized and market-relevant.

You need to edit your extensive design development in order to collate a coherent, balanced, and harmonious collection. Pulling out sketches and putting them together as a collection lineup with relevant fabric cuttings and colors will enable you to visualize and analyze the range in full. You may need to make subtle changes to color, fabrics, details, and outfit combinations in order to create a consistent and refined final look.

As a general rule, the silhouette will give the collection its key identity. For example, if square shoulders and nipped-in high waists determine the silhouette, this feature should run throughout the collection in some form.

Marie Pranning
A page from this menswear designer's sketchbook shows how she methodically works out all the information needed to create a successful collection. Within the lineup, each outfit has its own notes and allocated fabrics. Photographs and sketches of key elements help Marie to make decisions and remain focused.

Too many different silhouettes within one collection will be confusing and make the overall collection feel disjointed. At the same time, applying a surprise element within the collection, such as a print, texture, or textile embellishment, helps give the work a new dimension and creative depth, and keeps the collection from looking too regimented and uniform.

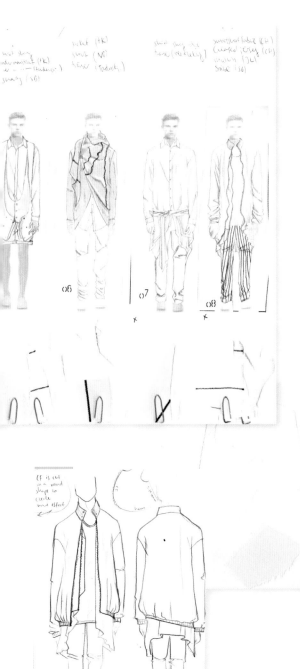

Presenting design proposals

Each project has its own distinct character and appeal. When presenting a collection to clients, the design team, or to tutors, the work should represent the overall theme and personality of the collection. Presenting work with similarities in layout and drawings will not distinguish the appropriateness of one project from another, resulting in a routine outcome.

As a general rule for presenting a collection you should have:

• Mood boards to represent the concept, color, fabrics, theme, customer, and market level.

• A drawn figurative lineup of front and back views in full color with accessories and styling details. This will show a collection or range clearly as one body of work. Relevant fabrics can be placed alongside each outfit.

• Spec drawings or working drawings help to identify key aspects within garments, such as seams, details, stitching, and cut. These are industry-specific, and provide

technical blueprints of each garment. They provide important information that can be easily read and understood by pattern cutters, sample machinists, and manufacturing units.

Fashion illustrations can be used to set the mood and promote the spirit of a collection. (Note that there is a clear distinction between fashion illustration and fashion drawing: the latter is used to sketch, refine, and communicate design ideas; the former is used to promote and set the scene.) Illustrations might depict a character with certain facial expressions, hair, make-up, and styling. A particular pose or stance might demonstrate an attitude that represents the look.

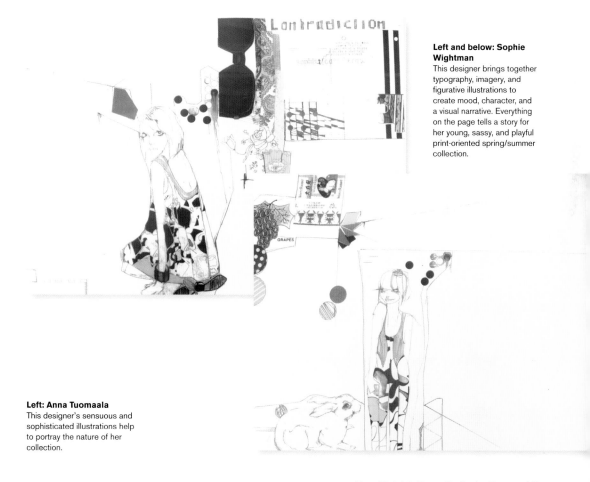

Left and below: Sophie Wightman
This designer brings together typography, imagery, and figurative illustrations to create mood, character, and a visual narrative. Everything on the page tells a story for her young, sassy, and playful print-oriented spring/summer collection.

Left: Anna Tuomaala
This designer's sensuous and sophisticated illustrations help to portray the nature of her collection.

The toile

A toile is the first 3D test to be carried out in the design process. The toile helps to create the shape of the garment in fabric and establish a definitive pattern for the final cutting and making stage.

Toiles are normally made in muslin (known as calico in the UK). This is a cheap cotton fabric that comes in various weights. It has a natural color (off-white), so it can easily be marked up with specific details or alterations. Muslin is a good substitute for most fabrics, however, designs that have a stretch element need to be toiled in a stretch fabric, such as jersey.

The toile allows the designer to make alterations and solve technical and manufacturing issues such as construction and fit. Although toiling is a technical exercise, it should remain creative. Most designers go straight into stand work from their research and use the 3D information to explore the 2D design development alongside the 3D toiling. Draping and sculpting on the stand allows the designer to see the design in real form and highlights important visual information that a drawing cannot supply, such as scale, shape, and an overall 3D view.

If the design has specific features, such as a neck detail or a complex shoulder shape, these areas can be toiled separately. Different versions at different scales can be made and then adapted to suit the outfit. These separate toiled features might be applied to other garments; this will bring a sense of uniformity to the overall collection or range.

Opposite: Calum Harvey
Photographs of toiles are judged against initial drawings. This helps menswear designer Calum Harvey to establish the overall look for his collection.

Right: Sian Lendrum
Sian Lendrum's first toile helps to visualize her complicated asymmetric dress. She will then analyze the toile in depth, making sure the fit, balance, line, and proportions are all correct. The toile will help answer many questions, such as the best techniques for manufacturing and the most appropriate fabric to use.

Toile fittings on models are essential. This is an opportunity to define the look and achieve the right fit, proportions, detail placement, and silhouette. Once all the garments have been toiled, a toile lineup with models is used to finalize the overall 3D look. The designer, the pattern cutter, sample machinist, and, if the budget allows, a stylist will make up the team that scrutinizes the collection. Original and alternative fabrics, drawings, and trims should all be at hand to be judged against the toiled outfits. Changes may then be made to fabrics and details, and some garments may be dropped and replaced so the collection maintains a harmonious rhythm and balance, while remaining appropriate to the brief and market level.

Once the team has made the alterations and finalized the toiles, the pattern cutter will draft out the final patterns for production in the final fabric.

As a general rule:
• Remain creative.
• Stand back and assess the shape of the toile from every angle. Remember to judge the proportions, line, silhouette, and the overall balance.
• Have a swatch of the real fabric near by so you can feel and assess the handle and quality in relation to the final design and silhouette.

Careers in Fashion

From designer endorsements to television shows like *Sex and the City*, the media spotlight falls on fashion more than ever before. The internet has brought about instant access to fashion from every perspective. These factors have contributed to making the fashion industry accessible to the general public. Working in the fashion industry is now considered a credible career, in contrast to the prevailing attitudes and presumptions in the 1970s and 80s.

Fashion's increased global recognition has led to the growth of many opportunities and varying career paths. However, along with the openings, it has also increased the number of people entering the industry and hence increased competition for jobs.

If you are considering a career in fashion, ask yourself: what do I want to achieve? What part do I want to play? Do I want to be a designer or a marketing manager? What market level do I want to work in? How do I go about it?

This chapter helps to answer these questions and highlights some of the routes available to get your career up and running.

College and university courses

Although designers such as Vivienne Westwood, Ralph Lauren, Catherine Walker, Chanel, and Rei Kawakubo had no formal training in fashion, they are exceptions to the rule. Nearly all reputable designers today have an undergraduate or postgraduate degree in fashion.

The fashion sector offers a variety of jobs, from creative and technical careers through to the business side of the industry. Colleges and universities internationally offer a variety of courses to cater for this need, such as Fashion Design, Fashion Marketing, Fashion Promotion, and combined degrees

Jess Au
Print designer Jess Au won the prestigious gold prize at the UK's Graduate Fashion Week in 2008. She gained vital skills and exposure at college, helping to launch her career in fashion.

such as Fashion with Business Studies. These courses can be the launch pad for a career in this increasingly competitive industry. Degree courses provide you with an opportunity to be exposed to the skills and processes that are needed to be successful. They also give you an important insight into the industry in its entirety. The reality is that not all graduates will become stars, but the training will arm you with the right tools to enter the industry in some capacity. Furthermore, a degree will provide prospective employers with an authoritative indication of your ability and commitment.

Entering fashion without formal training, prior knowledge, or contextual understanding will mean going in blind. This could leave you in the wilderness for years

Leading colleges and universities for fashion

United States
Academy of Art University (San Francisco, California)
Brooks College of Fashion (California)
Fashion Institute of Design and Merchandising (Los Angeles, San Francisco, San Diego)
Fashion Institute of Technology (FIT) (New York)
Otis College of Art and Design (Los Angeles)
Parsons The New School For Design (New York)
Pratt Institute (New York)

United Kingdom
Central Saint Martins College of Art and Design (London)
Kingston University (London)
London College of Fashion (London)
Northumbria University (Newcastle)
Nottingham Trent University (Nottingham)
Ravensbourne College of Design and Communication (London)
Royal College of Art (London)
University of Westminster (London)

Europe
Flanders Fashion Institute (Belgium)
Royal Academy of Fine Arts (Belgium)
Chambre Syndicale Fashion School (France)
IFM (Institut Français de la Mode) (France)
Accademia di Costume e Moda (Italy)
Domus Academy (Italy)
Istituto Marangoni (Italy)
Polimoda International Institute Fashion Design and Marketing (Italy)
Arnhem Academy of Art and Design (Netherlands)

Rest of the world
Royal Melbourne Institute of Technology (Australia)
National Institute of Fashion Technology (India)
Pearl Academy of Fashion (India)
Mode Gakuen (Japan)
Osaka Sogo College of Design (Japan)
LaSalle International Design School/ Raffles Design Institute (Malaysia, Singapore, China)

before you know exactly what you want. Before applying for any course, make sure you understand exactly what the course entails. All colleges and universities have open days for their courses; this is a great opportunity to get a taste of the atmosphere and for you to ask questions and speak to staff and students directly.

Below: Kasia Bishop
This designer's sketchbook pages show her experimental stand work. The sketchbook is an important place to record information; it helps to develop a line of enquiry and shows prospective colleges or employers your personal aesthetic.

Right: Laura Yiannakou
Laura Yiannakou creates an initial abstract composition within her sketchbook. This can be taken through and expanded into many different lines of enquiry, such as print.

The entry portfolio

As a candidate, your portfolio should be an extension of your creative personality. It should demonstrate a broad range of drawing skills, color knowledge and methods of execution, artistic awareness, and conceptualism. Sketchbooks are also very important. They should show your thought processes and your analysis, evaluation, and translation for each project. Be careful not to overload or overedit the content; remember that interviewees are looking for raw potential.

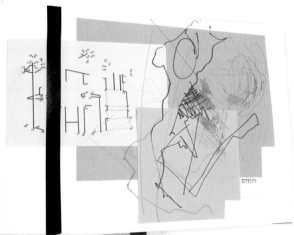

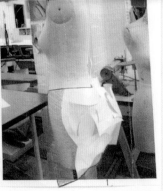

Right: Hannah Taylor
Hannah Taylor's sketchbook is energetic and experimental. Sketches show different perspectives and annotations, demonstrating in-depth enquiry and a passion for the subject matter.

Along with a portfolio review, tutors at colleges and universities may personally interview every candidate, so expressing your personality will be very important. You should be well informed and aware of current issues affecting the world and be able to articulate strong opinions and arguments. You will be expected to contextualize your work and the work of other artists and designers, so do not just live in a fashion bubble.

What to expect on the course

Expect a lot of hard work and plenty of healthy competition from fellow students. To succeed you will need to be committed, dedicated, have an open mind to acquire new skills and practices, and a thick skin to take on constructive criticism.

The structure of a syllabus is formulated in a sequential order, with each project acting as a building block for attaining new expertise and experience. Acquiring independence will be at the heart of every project, in preparation for the final year and a career in industry.

Students may feel the criticism is harsh, but I think it's possible they haven't had criticism before. It's my job to point out when something is badly done, or when there's no point of view. To build a brand you have to have something about you. If not personality, then some thought process. I'm forty, and they're young, so they're meant to be informing me. They should be bringing me a book or something that I haven't seen, not like some obscure chant book by Dominican monks, but an image of the way they see the world.

Louise Wilson, OBE, course leader in MA Fashion, Central Saint Martins College of Art and Design (London)

First-year projects aim to give students a broad introduction to practices such as design and research, fashion illustration, pattern cutting, and making real garments. This will expose the student to silhouette, proportion, color, and fabric, and their relationship within fashion design.

Most courses have womenswear, menswear, and fashion textiles projects; this helps the student decide what area they would like to specialize in. The contextual studies unit plays an important part in every course; it discusses the history of fashion and art, the theory of fashion, and how fashion can be put into a cultural context. By the end of the second year, students will have started to write their dissertation.

The second year is more challenging; greater emphasis is placed on the industry and professional practice. Projects are usually longer and have more direction, which enables the student to explore design, research, and presentation in greater depth. Students are encouraged to take part in national and international competitions. Some projects will be set by designers, big design houses, or retailers. This is a great opportunity for students to engage with industry, specialist tutors, and designers.

Work experience or an internship is a key feature of any course and may allow the student to consider working abroad. This allows the student to experience at first hand the industry in its true light, and usually takes place during or at the end of the second year. The time spent in industry can be negotiable; in most cases the experience can vary from three to six months. The exposure is helpful in making contacts and associations with companies and also in identifying and evaluating your own strengths and weaknesses. The placement usually culminates in a written work placement report.

The final year culminates in the production of a graduating collection consisting of six to eight outfits. This project has an open brief and gives the student total control of the outcomes; therefore design direction, research, management, analysis, and translation is in the student's hands.

Fittings and reviews with specialist tutors help the student to remain focused and achieve their aims and objectives. Therefore, the third year is based on preparing the student to enter the industry as a professional. Greater emphasis is given to developing an individual aesthetic and formulating an exciting and original portfolio of work.

One mustn't underestimate creativity or think of watertight compartments. You need to be able to sew, but also know about the history of art and architecture. Clothes are the result of things going on around them.
Maria Luisa Frisa, Fashion course director at IUAV (Venice)

Opposite: Graduate Fashion Week
Final-year students from Ravensbourne College (UK) present their highly accomplished collections at Graduate Fashion Week in London. This exposure gives students the opportunity to show off their skills in front of the national and international press and, most importantly, prospective employers from the major fashion houses.

The year ends with a fashion show. This is a great opportunity for students to show off their talents to the industry and prospective employers, and a chance to win awards and possibly gain some national or even international press coverage. Many notable designers have launched their careers from these final-year events, including John Galliano, Alexander McQueen, Stella McCartney, Marc Jacobs, and Bernhard Willhelm.

The students have to be individuals. If you don't have your own vision, you can't make collections. Clothes can be profound because they are an expression of the person who makes them.
Linda Loppa, former course director at the Royal Academy of Fine Arts (Antwerp)

The exit portfolio

Upon graduation, your exit portfolio will include a compilation of projects and competition work. The purpose of the portfolio is to demonstrate your skills, creativity, and ability to deliver professional, coherent work. The portfolio should be presented in such a way that it promotes your personal identity, and is able to entice prospective employers or clients.

The content and order of projects is important; instant impact can create excitement and interest in your work. The first project should be your strongest, and the portfolio should end with the second strongest piece of work. In between these, you should include projects that display a variety of skills such as good sense of color, line, spatial awareness, a personal aesthetic, and a sound understanding of fabrics. Overall presentation should be clear, consistent, relevant, and original.

The internet can be a great promotional tool. Having your own website can be a way to get yourself noticed, and there are many online portfolio websites to which you can upload your work. Employers are also increasingly using Facebook to headhunt potential employees.

Prepare for interviews with prospective companies or designers by researching and understanding their aesthetic and market level. Don't be afraid to edit or add projects that seem appropriate to their work. After the interview, always leave the interviewer with a reminder of you and your work. This could be a small creative package, postcard, CD or DVD, or simply a resumé and a business card.

Life after graduation

Every year thousands of students graduate with a fashion-related degree, but there is only a limited number of jobs available. With fashion colleges in all major cities across the globe, the number of graduates with fashion degrees can easily be tripled.

This sounds like a daunting prospect, so upon graduating you should be open to every possibility. Ask yourself: where do I fit in? Who do I want to work for? How do I get my foot in the door? How do I go about achieving my aims? Be prepared to transfer knowledge to other creative sectors such as graphic design or costume design; this will help you to bide some time and enhance your skill levels. Make a checklist of your skills. Be honest; ask yourself, do I struggle with design? Am I a better pattern cutter than a designer? Is my interpretation of

All images: Arsida Smajili
This designer's final portfolio pages show a professional and clear presentation. The aesthetic stays true to the designer's collection and her personal approach to fashion.

color and fabric strong or weak? This will point up areas where you could improve your skills, or make you consider jobs you hadn't thought of before. Being a sample machinist, for example, should not be considered to be a step down. A technically superior sample machinist is worth their weight in gold. Within the industry their reputation spreads like wild fire and they become legends in their own right. They can solve design and technical issues saving the designer time and money, hence becoming an important asset within the team.

As with many creative jobs, the way in is often to get an internship or work experience placement. Most companies are willing to take on graduates from three months to up to a year. This is valuable experience; it will help to reaffirm your skills and your desire to be in the industry and give you the opportunity to acquire new skills, take on new challenges, and impress an employer or designer with a view to being offered a permanent paid position.

Setting up an independent label

A number of graduates decide to go it alone, either working freelance for various companies or setting up their own independent label. Working freelance has its advantages: it gives you independence; in most cases you are able to work from home; you work on a variety of projects as opposed to constantly working for one company, and the work can be well paid. However, there are also the disadvantages of finding the clients and ensuring you have enough work all year round to make it worthwhile. At some point you may have to manage two or three projects at a time—you really can't say no or pick and choose. In addition there is the strong possibility of irregular income; you may get paid for two projects one month and for the next six weeks not have a project at all. Therefore, contacts, self-promotion, and good time management are essential if you are to succeed.

Setting up an independent fashion label is not for everyone. Before you get swept away by the glamor of having your own

front view line up

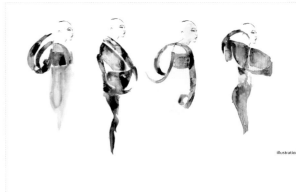

illustratio

label, you need to ask yourself why you want to do it. Are you able to offer something new to the market? Can you afford to go it alone? If your answer is yes, then ask yourself; do I have the desire, self-belief, business acumen, and skills necessary? Am I prepared to work long hours? Certainly for the first few years live with financial insecurity? Most importantly, have I got the will to succeed no matter what?

Having your own label enables you to explore and produce your design ideas, and gives you sole authority for the creative direction. Designers such as John Galliano, Alexander McQueen, and Marios Schwab, to name but a few, have used their labels as a launch pad to promote their work and personal design aesthetic to attract the big jobs in fashion—Galliano at Dior, McQueen at Givenchy, and Marios Schwab relaunching the US label Halston. Other designers, such as Jonathan Saunders, have designed ranges for mass-market retailers, or provided their skills to various companies or conglomerates as consultants or creative directors. In this way revenue can be generated to support the independent label.

The disadvantages of independence are many, including the long hours, constant financial pressures, and time spent chasing people for money. The continuous stresses of managing the studio can lead to low morale and affect the creative nature of the business. If the label has financial backers, your independence can become compromised. In a worst-case scenario, if the label fails to make money or fails to meet its orders, investors can decide to withdraw their financial backing, leaving the label bankrupt. Such was the case for designer Luella Bartley in 2009; her label was unable to fulfil its orders for spring/summer 2010 due to production problems. This resulted in her backers pulling their financial support, leaving the designer with no choice but to close the business.

If you do decide to go it alone, financial backing is essential. The setting up and running costs of a studio, the manufacturing process, the hiring of specialist staff such as pattern cutters and sample machinists, and having a fashion show season after season to promote your work are all very expensive. Investors will need to see a detailed business plan before they make any financial commitments. Consider all the possibilities and the financial implications carefully. But first ask yourself: do I have the mental and physical strength to succeed?

Be prepared for knockbacks. Be realistic and honest with your aims, keep updating your portfolio, identify your weaknesses, and do something positive to keep on improving. Above all, never lose faith in your ability!

Fashion jobs to consider

- Assistant designer
- Designer
- Fashion buyer
- Fashion forecaster
- Fashion illustration
- Fashion journalist
- Fashion merchandiser
- Fashion photographer
- Fashion PR
- Fashion show producer or organizer
- Knitwear designer
- Museum curator
- Pattern cutter/creative pattern cutter
- Print designer
- Production manager
- Sample machinist
- Stylist
- Tailor
- Visual merchandiser

Amus Leung
Amus Leung's creative package includes a business card, a resumé, a press statement, illustrations, and a foldout look book of her collection. A creative package is a great way to generate interest in your work and to remind perspective employers or press of your creative credentials.

Portfolios

From wacky catwalk shows and glamorous glossy magazines, to commercially led fashion brands in shopping malls, fashion as an industry has become an overwhelming international creative force. The power of fashion in all its guises has played a major role in shaping modern culture and, in some way or another, it consciously or unconsciously affects us all on a personal level.

Some designers have worked with the simple goal of providing clothes as a necessity. Others have set out to challenge every conventional notion concerned with clothing, questioning identity, beauty, artifice, and gender. This intellectual and commercial mix of ideas and the highly-charged philosophical debates conducted via design have produced fashion practitioners with many idiosyncratic talents.

This portfolio section highlights some of the world's most influential and creative designers working today. Each has an individual method of working and putting forward their design aesthetic. Some have become global brands, while others have remained independent, resisting the lure of global commercialization and remaining true to their creative beliefs.

It is hoped that each portfolio experience will help to inspire the reader to encounter the fashion industry at first hand.

Marc Jacobs
One of the world's leading fashion designers, Marc Jacobs runs his own successful label as well as holding the position of Creative Director at Louis Vuitton.

Viktor & Rolf

"We're not inspired directly by fabrics or materials; we're more conceptual. We like to tell a story, we try to think of what we want to say at this moment, comment on how we feel at this moment in time. In that sense it's more like a story or an anecdote or a mood."

Highly creative and conceptual, the Dutch design duo Viktor Horsting and Rolf Snoeren are regarded as master tacticians of fashion's semiotic narrative. Image and presentation are fundamental to their work. "Fashion doesn't have to be something people wear," they say; "fashion is also an image." Unlike Comme des Garçons or Martin Margiela, who base their avant-garde aesthetic on deconstruction, Viktor & Rolf create a playful arena of fantasy and fairy tales. Since their early couture collections, they have developed a refined primness and referential approach. Parisian fashion's decorative and clichéd details such as frills and pussycat bows are now part of every collection, along with a play on the classic tuxedo and white shirt.

Like the British fine artists Gilbert and George, Viktor & Rolf look the same, dress the same, and present themselves as one of a kind. The two forged their partnership while studying fashion at Arnhem Academy of Art and Design in the Netherlands. After graduating in 1992, they immediately moved to Paris to carve out a career in fashion's most prestigious capital. While working on their own designs they also undertook internships at established labels such as Maison Martin Margiela and Jean Colonna.

Working from their tiny apartment in Paris, Viktor & Rolf designed and produced their first collection in 1993. It was based on their personal experience of feeling alienated in the foreign city. They created a collection of ten looks examining reconstruction via extreme silhouettes and the application of multiple layers of cut-up old shirts and suits that dwarfed the body. More akin to performance art than fashion, they produced a dress from scratch and then subjected it to destructive experiments: slamming it in a door, cutting it, burning it. Their conceptual ideas of distortion, exaggerated proportions, and unique presentation of fashion and form won the duo three first prizes at the Salon Europeen des Jeunes Stylistes at the Festival International de Mode et de Photographie in France. For the next five years, Viktor & Rolf continued to present their experimental and artistic fashion via exhibitions and installations.

Black Hole ready-to-wear collection, fall/winter 2001/02
Inspired by shadows, this collection was entirely black. The models were given blacked-out faces, giving prominence to the tailored silhouette and exaggerated details.

Left: There's No Business Like Show Business ready-to-wear collection, spring/summer 2001
Based on American sportswear as well as playing on masculine and feminine tailoring, this catwalk show was presented as a musical performance with Busby Berkeley-like formations. Viktor & Rolf joined the models for the final tap dance.

Above: Harlequin ready-to-wear collection, spring/summer 2008
In this presentation, models emerged through the wide-open mouth of an enlarged black-and-white photograph of celebrity model Shalom Harlow.

experiencing severe financial constraints under German occupation took innovative steps to keep their businesses going: they created miniature collections that were presented on dolls. These dolls traveled the world to show potential clients the couturiers' latest work. Viktor & Rolf drew on this tradition in 1996 when, penniless and back in the Netherlands, working and living in Amsterdam, they presented their Launch collection on dolls in the Torch Gallery. The installation included a mini-design studio, catwalk, photoshoot, boutique, and the modern-day symbol of every successful fashion label—a limited-edition perfume. Although the perfume was totally fictitious, Viktor & Rolf staged a real glossy promotional ad photographed by Wendelien Daan, which went on to be published in *V* magazine. The pair later commented, "the scent's intoxicating effect could only ever be imagined." Launch encapsulated the duo's vision, dreams, and aspirations for the future, but most importantly gave them an opportunity to trial their provocative self-promotion and manipulation of their satirical vision of fashion and image.

Left: Monsieur menswear line, spring/summer 2008
Viktor & Rolf's menswear line replicates the duo's own image. This model wears a gradated print tailored suit, accessorized with nerdy black-framed glasses, similar to those worn by the designer pair.

In 1998, Launch became reality. Victor & Rolf became the first Dutch guest members invited by the Chambre Syndicale de la Couture Parisienne to show their collection as part of Paris haute couture week. The spring/summer collection was a reflective study and homage to couture. Integral elements associated with couture such as luxury fabric, color, embroidery, accessories, ornamentation, and craftsmanship were the basis for their first runway collection. The collection was in keeping with the pair's unorthodox and inverted aesthetic; for example, a coat dress in luxurious silk incorporated a traditional embroidery ring creating a sculptural silhouette and displaying exquisite embellishment that was left unfinished, thereby celebrating the dexterity of haute couture.

The show also provided Viktor & Rolf with an opportunity to explore performance as a vehicle for presenting fashion on the runway. Against a background soundtrack, which repeated "Viktor & Rolf" in different voices, each model stood motionless on a plinth to reflect the historical importance of couture and stood as a testimony to couture's superior status within fashion.

Right: Harlequin ready-to-wear spring/ summer 2008 collection. Inspired by Man Ray's surrealist photograph *Ingres's Violin*, Viktor & Rolf present a pink, double-faced silk organza coat with a white silk organza cabbage-rose corsage. Embedded into the oversized trademark ruffles

"We were drawn to couture and its symbolic function. In fashion it is the top of the pyramid, the *ne plus ultra* of luxury. It also functions as a laboratory without commercial restraints. Couture is like a sacred realm outside reality—a notion we are quite inspired by."

Viktor & Rolf's second couture collection, AtomicBomb, for fall/winter 1998/99, was highly acclaimed for its spectacular theatrical presentation and the beautiful sensitivity of drapery and volume. Based on the silhouette of the mushroom cloud created by the atomic bomb, garments were either stuffed with balloons or padded out with silk and then shown again without the exaggerated implants that created a new silhouette. Like their earlier conceptual projects, the duo's subsequent couture collections, Black Light (spring/summer 1999), Russian Doll (fall/winter 1999/2000), and Bells fall/winter 2000/01) have been arenas for experimentation. With very little commercial success, these garments have become artistic masterpieces that have received critical acclaim from various fashion commentators and taken center stage at numerous worldwide exhibitions.

r & Rolf have continued to wow the
ion world with their surreal vision.
dy-to-wear collections such as Black
e (fall/winter 2001/02), Long Live the
aterial (fall/winter 2002), One Woman
w (fall/winter 2003/04), Bedtime Story
winter 2005/06), and The Fashion Show
winter 2007/08) have all helped to push
boundaries and become seminal
ments within contemporary fashion.
y have also contributed to the menswear
lution by launching their menswear line
003. The line, called Monsieur, is a
ection of the duo's own image—classic
with a dash of humor.
005 represented one of the most
ortant periods in Viktor & Rolf's career.
ngside their spring/summer collection,
werbomb, they launched their first
al" perfume, also called Flowerbomb,
ollaboration with L'Oréal. In April 2005,
y opened their first independent
tique, on Milan's Via Sant'Andrea.
signed by architect Siebe Tettero, the
p is based on a classic French boutique.
opulent neoclassical interior bears the
marks of a Viktor & Rolf performance; all
furniture and fittings hang upside down.

distinctly unconventional yet visually
beautiful, intellectual, and compelling
atmosphere. Although inspired by a radical
approach toward scale and presenting an
escape from reality, their research always
takes classicism as a starting point. By
taking what already exists, they twist and
reshape their fashion product within Viktor
& Rolf's very own fantasy world.

Important collaborations with Samsonite
for a luggage range, Shu Uemura for a range
of couture false eyelashes, and their highly
publicized sell-out collection for H&M
have furthered Viktor & Rolf's wider
market appeal.

**The Fashion Show
ready-to-wear collection,
fall/winter 2007/08**
Viktor & Rolf took the idea
of the fashion show and
its accouterments as the
conceptual starting point for
this collection. Each model
and outfit is a self-sufficient

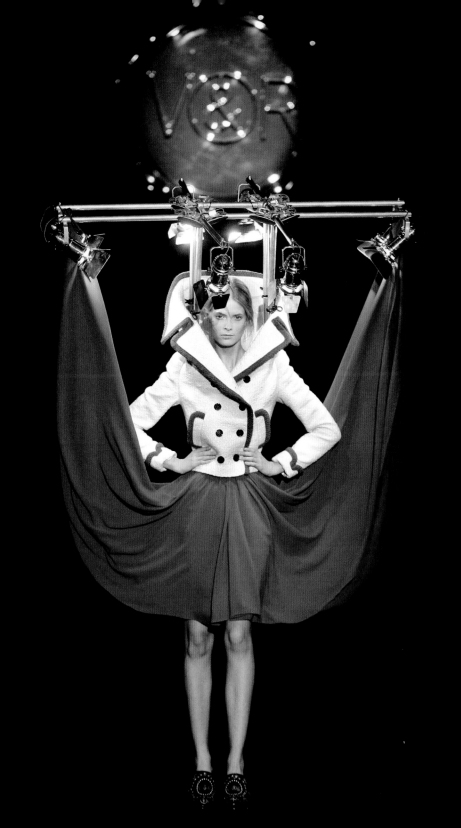

Boudicca

"What we've always lived by is—form follows emotion."

The English label Boudicca features the design partnership of Zowie Broach and Brian Kirkby. They take their name and inspiration from the queen of the Iceni, who showed strength in the face of adversity and led her tribe against the Roman imperial forces who were occupying Britain in 60AD. The label shares the queen's bloody-mindedness and fearless, uncompromising passion. Boudicca's fashion is impeccably made with dextrous attention; every seam, every detail is meticulously scrutinized before it leaves the studio.

Formed in 1997, Boudicca present collections that challenge the boundaries of fashion and make the wearer experience new emotions. With many financial constraints and unable to compete on the same platform as other established labels, they spent years in semi-obscurity. They showed in art galleries and other exhibition spaces for their first four years, until the British Fashion Council invited the duo to show at London Fashion Week in 2001.

The Tornado Dress, October 2009
A still from *The Tornado Dress*, a short film by Boudicca, directed by Ben Bannister.

oudicca stands for something rare in
shion: integrity and intelligence. An
ricate geometry that created streamlined
sign, incorporating elements of
coration, from surface with sheen on
ather to zippers raked askew."

zy Menkes, *International Herald Tribune*, **2003**

---

tially the label received mixed reviews
om the fashion pack, but the impact of
eir fall/winter collection in 2003 showed
eir intent. Each garment was cut and
ilored with precision in luxurious silks,
ools, and austere leather. The fashion
ess applauded and declared Boudicca the
ew avant-garde of British fashion. A new
urney for the label began with the award
British fashion's most serious prize, a
x-figure sponsorship deal from American
xpress. The only previous recipient of this
ward had been Alexander McQueen.
After showing in New York for three
easons, an invitation from the Chambre
yndicale to show during Paris haute
outure week in January 2007 gave the
bel an opportunity to express their
tention for purity of cut and line on
new level. The collection, called
orever—A Dream Sequence, embraced
he label's strongest facets. It featured
ng, dark, shimmering dresses and
nmaculate tailoring worn with wide belts
nd draped chains that referenced the
warrior queen herself. Boudicca was
he first independent British fashion
ouse to become a guest member of
he Chambre Syndicale.

The label's thoughtful and at times mind-
boggling research takes reference from
the surreal to the political. Their clothes and
catwalk presentations have a strong sense
of movie realism. Boudicca presents scenes
and sequences, panning in and out, in focus,
and then a blur. The title of each collection,
which can easily be attributed to a book or
movie, has an intense emotive meaning,
and, as with all good stories, their work
has a beginning, a middle, and a
provocative ending.

Boudicca's quest to question, expand,
and express enables them to pursue new
challenges. This gives them time to breathe
and take stock from the everyday
monotonous demands of fashion. They
challenge their creativity by taking part in
art exhibitions such as the Arnhem Mode
Biennale and collaborative projects. One
such project, organized by *Vogue* UK in
2004, saw Boudicca design a dress in
collaboration with British architect David
Adjaye, thereby bringing together the
aesthetics and practices of architecture and
couture. In another collaboration, Oscar-
nominated British filmmaker Mike Figgis
photographed Boudicca's first couture
collection. The resulting images were
exhibited at the Picture House Film, Art
and Design Gallery in the UK in 2007.

Wode
Promotional ad for Boudicca's
first "art" fragrance, launched
in September 2008.

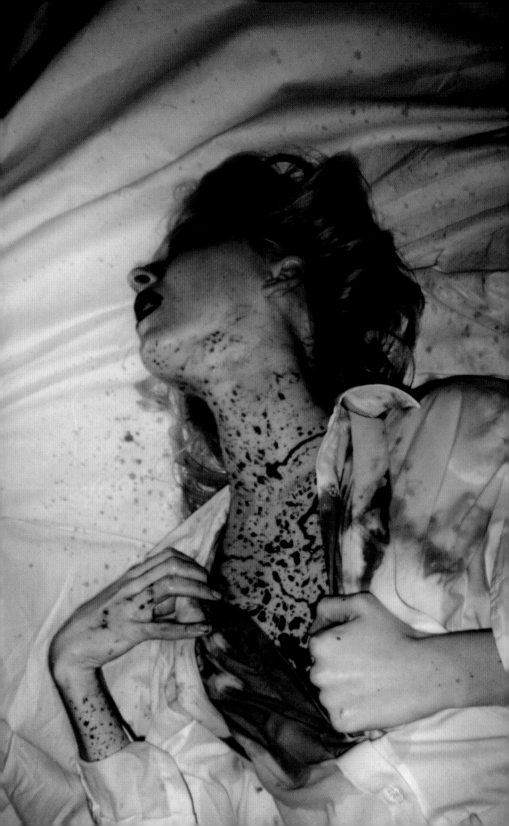

From experimental London to the commercial fashion capital of New York and then onto the ultimate arena of Parisian haute couture, Boudicca's journey has been one of discovery and challenges without compromise. The label continues its experimentation with Wode, the revolutionary art fragrance that took years to develop. The scent comes housed in a graffiti can; when it is sprayed on, a vibrant cobalt-blue mist settles on the skin or clothing and disappears within seconds, leaving behind just the scent. Legend has it that Queen Boudicca and her soldiers painted woad, a cobalt-blue dye, on their faces and bodies to intimidate the enemy before advancing into battle.

By combining technology with an artisan approach, the design duo behind Boudicca ask questions about identity and the relationship between the real and virtual. Through their answers they strive to push the boundaries of fashion even further. Boudicca remains a label for those who understand, not for the masses.

The Beautiful and the Insane ready-to-wear collection, spring/summer 2005
A battle helmet inspired this beautifully fashioned headpiece, which remains true to Queen Boudicca's warrior image.

Right: Forever–A Dream Sequence haute couture collection, spring/summer 2007
Boudicca present their first couture collection in Paris. Retaining their personal aesthetic, this beautifully constructed lace dress and draped shoulder accessory displays qualities associated with haute couture.

Opposite: Still haute couture collection, spring/summer 2008
Boudicca throw the glamorous haute couture ideal to one side and put forward their modern and strong vision for a black evening dress.

would have done things
, but I want to create something
nt to suggest to people different
s and values. I want to question
g."

in fashion, yet revered as one of
eminent designers of our time, Rei
designs clothes that are original
rd-thinking in every sense. Her
ox approach to the body, fabric,
olor, and silhouette for both
wear and menswear makes
s the preferred choice of those
to look independent and make
tatement.

aduate of the fine arts and
Kawakubo's avant-garde and
pproach bears the hallmarks of an
al background. After working briefly
and as a stylist, Kawakubo started
clothes under the label Comme
ns in 1969. The name itself is
, translating as "Like the Boys."
ommentators and theorists alike
erated on its political and sexual
stics, yet it was simply chosen
Kawakubo liked the sound of it.
her clothes are frequently
lized and associated with modern

artist she denies such connections.
"My approach is simple," she claims;
result is something other people decid

In 1981, Kawakubo took to the wor
stage in dramatic fashion. Kawakubo a
her fellow Japanese designer Yohji
Yamamoto were the first foreign desig
invited to show their collections in Par
Kawakubo's showcase of oversized
silhouettes, frayed edges, knitted tops
punctured with intentional random ho
and a stark color palette of just black v
a seminal moment in fashion history t
shocked the Parisian establishment.
Accustomed to a diet of bourgeois off
from Chanel and Dior, critics found it c
to understand and contextualize the
concept; they labeled the collection
"Hiroshima Chic" and "Japanese bag
look," much to Kawakubo's distaste. E
mid-1980s, however, most of the majo
boutiques across Europe were stockir
collections. As *Vogue* pointed out; "if
European observer felt at odds with th
look, the European wearer did not." A
decade later, the very same androgyn
lived-in look was the instigator of grun
fashion that manifested itself into read
wear and haute couture fashion. By th
Kawakubo had already moved on crea

Ready-to-wear collection, fall/winter 2008/09
Different sizes of hexagons are brought together to create a voluminous unstructured silhouette. The extravagant headpiece serves not only as a spectacle, but also helps to lengthen and exaggerate the image of the body.

Kawakubo's creative process is centered on the concept of form and beauty. By juxtaposing elements of urban decay, luxury, and tradition she is able to achieve a deconstruction of the norm, a new category in which, she explains, "the body becomes dress becomes body." In doing so, conventional proportions and configurations of openings, pockets, collars, sleeves, and trimmings take on a new character and design aesthetic that questions the role of the body and Western notions of adorned beauty. She once made a dress without any openings, making it impossible to put on. Insisting that it could be worn, Kawakubo declared that it could be tied to the body like an apron. Her infamous Bump collection from 1997 outlined her fascination with form. Female body parts such as the waist, stomach, and buttocks were manipulated by padding and sculpting new, exaggerated shapes on top of the existing body, thereby dismantling the observer's traditional view of the female image.

Ready-to-wear collection, fall/winter 2008
Kawakubo's playful and childlike ingenuity brings together an outfit that juxtaposes elements of traditional menswear and sweet, childlike floral prints and color references.

Kawakubo's radical approach extends to her business organization, which explores new ideas and innovative retail strategies and collaborations. Recruiting designers such as Junya Watanabe, Tao Kurihara, and Ganryu, she has set up her very own Comme des Garçons think tank. Each contributor designs individual lines for the label as well as receiving support to pursue their own independent collections. In addition, notable collaborations have taken place with Levis, Lacoste, Fred Perry, H&M, and Speedo.

The Comme des Garçons shops are as revolutionary in concept and execution as the collections. They range from guerrilla stores and black stores that have limited lifespans and destinations, to a flagship store in London's Dover Street Market, which houses handpicked designer labels alongside the Comme des Garçons brand.

After forty years, Rei Kawakubo continues to influence not only the general world of fashion, but also notable individual designers such as Martin Margiela and Ann Demeulemeester. She presents her collections in Paris four times a year and still has the ability to shock and leave the fashion press in sheer wonderment, if not a little bewildered.

Far right: Ready-to-wear collection, spring/summer 2008
"Clusters," "randomness," and "cacophony" are the words used by Rei Kawakubo to explain her inspiration. The model's face is here made up to resemble a clown, and the dress looks like a naïve cutout silhouette found in a children's activity book.

Right: Ready-to-wear collection, spring/summer 2008
In Rei Kawakubo's world, a tailored jacket can become part of a skirt, adding a new complex dimension to what was a rather routine skirt.

**Ready-to-wear collection,
spring/summer 2007**
This deconstructed
high-belted jacket is
reconnected with sheer mesh,
overlays of organza, and white
plastic. The ballerina skirt
bears a Japanese red disc,
a cultural reference to
Kawakubo's place of origin,
but also signifying the purity
of the red dot.

**Opposite: Homme Plus
menswear collection,
fall/winter 2009/10**
Kawakubo's menswear vision
is a quirky mix of traditional
and English-inspired fashion
for men.

**Left: Homme Plus
menswear collection,
spring/summer 2010**
Here the traditional tie takes
on a new persona; instead of
being tied around the neck,
several ties are brought
together to make the front
façade of a tailored jacket.
With a suggestion of a skirt
over pants, the suit is
transformed, thereby
questioning male identity.

Rei Kawakubo 157

Left: Junya Watanabe for Comme des Garçons, ready-to-wear collection, fall/winter 2006/07
This designer stays true to the Comme des Garçons look, but adds his own flavor to the collection.

Right: Ready-to-wear collection, fall/winter 2009/10
A deconstructed silhouette and questions about beauty and identity are hallmarks of Rei Kawakubo's challenging aesthetic.

Walter Van Beirendonck

"I have a love/hate relationship with fashion, because I'm not so fond of the superficial [nature of it]. For me, it's very important that there is always content, something that should be told."

A fashion student from the renowned Royal Academy of Fine Arts in Antwerp, Belgium, Walter Van Beirendonck graduated with the enigmatic Martin Margiela in 1980. The following year the graduates included Dries Van Noten, Ann Demeulemeester, Dirk Bikkembergs, Dirk Van Saene, and Marina Yee. Even as a student, Van Beirendonck's individual stance on fashion stood out. While his contemporaries were preoccupied with creating a new deconstructed aesthetic, he was more interested in outlandish, extravagant, futuristic colorways and male silhouettes more akin to comic-book superheroes.

Van Beirendonck launched his first signature line in 1983, but it was not until 1987 at the British Designer Show in London that the Flemish designer made his most important breakthrough. As one of the "Antwerp Six" along with Van Noten, Demeulemeester, Bikkembergs, Van Saene, and Yee, Van Beirendonck affirmed his very personal vision for menswear fashion in front of a packed international fashion audience.

Right: Explicit collection, spring/summer 2009
The male body, muscles, and body parts are an important inspiration for this collection, as well as freedom and nature. This model wears a beard made from leaves and a transparent suit that reveals printed body parts.

Below: Explicit collection, spring/summer 2009
Fabrics that look like plastic and bubble wrap are in fact high-quality silk-based materials. Blow-up features around the shoulders and upper arms add a 3D element to the concept of muscles.

Right: Explicit collection, spring/summer 2009
The natural body is exposed in contrast to the manmade printed muscles.

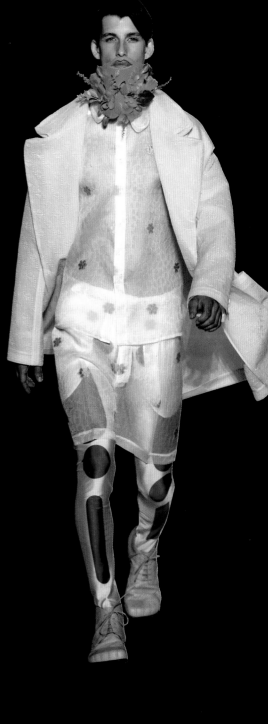

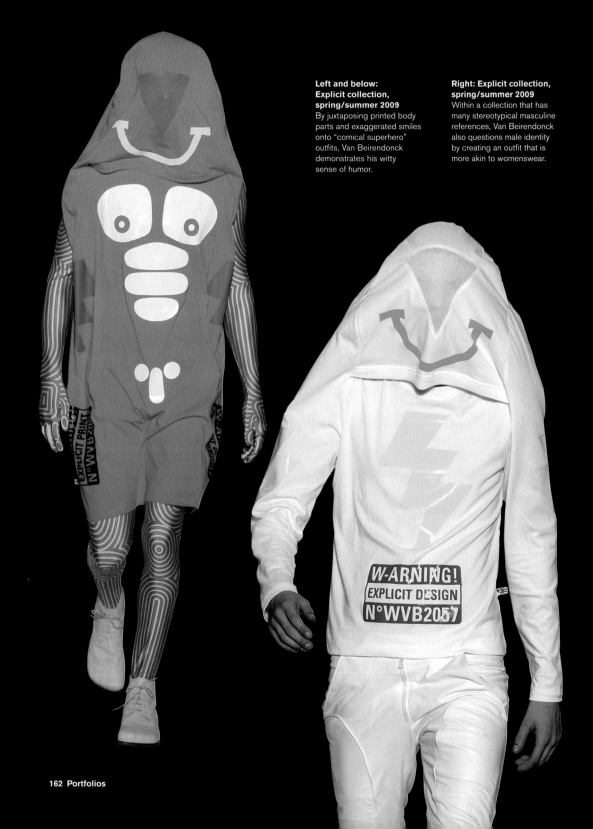

**Left and below:
Explicit collection,
spring/summer 2009**
By juxtaposing printed body
parts and exaggerated smiles
onto "comical superhero"
outfits, Van Beirendonck
demonstrates his witty
sense of humor.

**Right: Explicit collection,
spring/summer 2009**
Within a collection that has
many stereotypical masculine
references, Van Beirendonck
also questions male identity
by creating an outfit that is
more akin to womenswear.

From 1993 to 1999, alongside his signature collection, Van Beirendonck also designed a more affordable line, W.&L.T. (Wild and Lethal Trash), in collaboration with German company Mustang. He explains, "Wild is obvious; lethal is something that can be over the top, like you are lethal in love. Trash stands for consumption and throwing away."

The W.&L.T collections were predominantly based around streetwear presented in ultramodern fabrics, garish cyber-punk colorways, graphic prints, and slogans concerning politics, sex, and nature. Silhouettes and outfits varied from wearable combat jackets and pants to latex all-in-one bodysuits. His fascination with cyber technology led the forward-thinking designer to launch W.&L.T. on the internet with a dedicated website and a full CD-ROM. Besides the collections, information and self-designed interactive games were a key feature. The website was the first online fashion label to experiment with this new media experience.

Overleaf: Explicit collection, spring/summer 2009
The finale brings together all the different elements associated with the theme for the collection as one body of work.

Van Beirendonck is inspired by everything around him. He has a passion for attaining knowledge from various sources, such as surfing the web, visiting museums and art galleries, going to libraries, and reading books on diverse subject matters from tribal ethnicity to debates on gender. "The themes for my collections come rather naturally; it's not because I suddenly want to do something. I'm always looking around, and at the same time I'm thinking about what's going on, and the themes that are interesting to me are popping up and are becoming a topic. At that moment I decide which idea is more important than the others. I select it and go for it, and luckily every season something happens that is interesting to bring forward as a subject for my collection."

In 1999, Van Beirendonck launched his Aestheticterrorists label. The line was a clear attack on the commercialized fashion world. Striking prints and in-your-face slogans such as "I Hate Fashion" and "Ban Fashion Nazis" made his opinion of the fashion marketing system very clear. "I don't accept that things should be done only for selling. It's really here [the collections] where I see my creativity and that's where I can express my creativity 100%." He goes on to say, "I keep on believing in creativity. I think after years when marketing was very dominant in fashion, I think we need an injection of creativity. I'm sure this creativity will make a difference in the future."

More futuristic than contemporary, his thought-provoking and visually humorous collections remain one of the highlights of Menswear Fashion Week in Paris.

Van Beirendonck continues to debate and present his vision of gender and masculinity in his own unique way. There are those who admire his work and creative aesthetic and others who find his work a joke; for some his fashion is vaguely disturbing. "I did 120 men covered in rubber latex and then on top I put the clothes. For me, the idea was an ecological statement. Some people saw it as a safe sex message. Others saw it as an S&M thing. So many interpretations—I was amazed!"

All images: Take a W-Ride collection, fall/winter 2010/11
Walter Van Beirendonck's customary superheroes, exaggerated accessories, full-on color, humor, traditional menswear, and sportswear dominate this collection.

His signature label, Walter Van Beirendonck, has stockists around the world, but primarily his collections are sold from his flagship store, Walter, in Antwerp. Designed in collaboration with the Australian industrial designer Marc Newson and Antwerp architectural firm B-Architecten, the store also provides hanger space for other designers including Dirk Van Saene, Bless, and Vexed Generation. The annex, called Window, is a gallery space that houses fashion, photography, and art exhibitions.

Van Beirendonck's enthusiastic creative spirit continues to expand and venture into other artistic arenas. He has designed costumes for theater, movies, and ballet. Not limited to the fashion world, he publishes the magazine *Wonder*, illustrates, and serves as a regular exhibition curator. As well as being an all-round creative, Walter Van Beirendonck is a respected academic. A visiting professor at the Royal Academy of Fine Arts, he has nurtured designer protégés including Bernhard Willhelm and Stephan Schneider.

Left: Glow collection, fall/winter 2009/10
Inspired by neon lighting, a traditional men's tailored jacket and bowler hat take on a new abstract perspective.

Right: Glow collection, fall/winter 2009/10
This knitted sweater is intricately constructed, in keeping with the neon lighting theme, to reveal a face similar to those seen in African art.

Hedi Slimane

"It's very important to try to understand the time you are living in, to be a part of the present. I always try to know the spirit of the time."

Menswear fashion is predictably built around rules, constraints, and tradition. However, every so often a special talent emerges who breaks the rules in order to echo and capture the moment. The appointment of Hedi Slimane as creative director at Christian Dior Monsieur in 2000 is seen as a defining moment in contemporary menswear fashion. Straight away he set out to define the new origins of Dior menswear by creating a new brand, Dior Homme, replacing Christian Dior Monsieur. Many fashion commentators and fellow creatives regard him as the designer who single-handedly brought about a revolution in modern menswear. "Hedi's attitude is right and what he does and designs is about attitude. From his generation, he expresses modernity better than any other menswear designer," says Karl Lagerfeld.

Unlike most young designers, Slimane did not study fashion at college; he read art history and political sciences at the École du Louvre. During his studies and after graduation in 1990, Slimane continued to work with his friend, French fashion designer José Levy, on a casual basis. He helped out with art direction for fashion shows, styling and casting models for shows, notably from the street. It was on the streets in 1987 that Slimane spotted a young French punk called Jérome Le Chevalie. He instantly photographed this skinny young man and put him in José Lévy's show. Jérome was the first "waif boy" model appearing in the late 1980s, in complete contrast to the usual muscular chisel-chinned models of the time.

Slimane then went on to assist Jean-Jacques Picard, making a notable contribution toward the centenary exhibition of Louis Vuitton's "LV" monogram in 1996.

In 1997, Pierre Berge (CEO of Yves Saint Laurent) appointed Slimane as collections and art director to relaunch Yves Saint Laurent Rive Gauche Homme. Not until 1999 did this role give Slimane his first taste of creative independence and authority. Inspired by Yves Saint Laurent's influential signature styles of the late 1960s and 70s, Slimane's first collections for the house made references to Le Smoking, Left Bank,

Dior Homme collection, fall/winter 2006/07
A slim and sharp silhouette was the hallmark of Dior menswear designed by Hedi Slimane. It set out to challenge the conventions of men's fashion and present a modern androgynous style.

and Safari Chic. Slim black tuxedos, leather shirts and jeans, and safari jackets with lace-front shirts steered away from being retro, but represented a new interpretation of modernity with a hint of androgyny.

"I think that Rive Gauche has always had a certain mystique," explains Slimane. "It seems to me that the foundations of the modern wardrobe were settled for good by Monsieur Saint Laurent in the late 1960s. I would like what I'm doing to be a mix of Paris, of couture, and of elegance."

While at YSL, Hedi Slimane attracted attention from the fashion world at large. On leaving YSL in 1999, Slimane was approached by the Gucci Group to finance his own brand and also by the Prada Group to take the reins at Jil Sander. Instead, Slimane took up LVMH's offer to become creative director of Christian Dior Monsieur in 2000. A tired menswear label that had previously concentrated on suits and ties and that had limited market distribution was to experience a significant overhaul. Continuing from where he left off at YSL, Slimane brought with him his slim and sharp androgynous silhouette. His creation, Dior Homme, was now in keeping with his ultramodern vision for menswear fashion. In 2002, the Council of Fashion Designers of America (CFDA) named him their international designer of the year.

Enthused by a fusion of music, fashion, and photography, Slimane worked closely with a number of British rock bands, including Franz Ferdinand, The Libertines, and in particular his divisive muse Pete Doherty of Babyshambles, in order to perfect his style for Dior Homme.

The Dior Homme look
Skinny, boyish-looking models are typical of the men used by Hedi Slimane to characterize the look for Dior Homme in promotional campaigns and catwalk presentations.

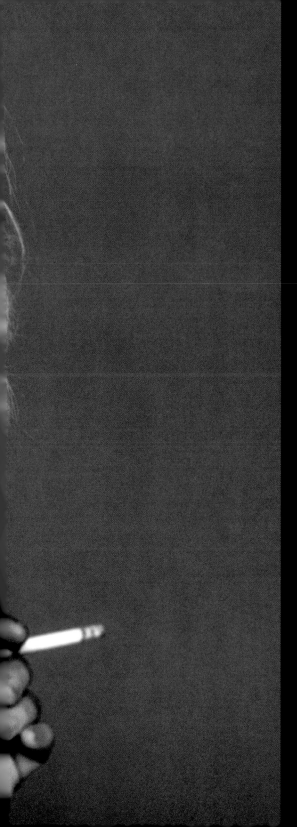

From 2000 to 2007, the Dior look was characterized by young, tall, punky, skinny boys recruited from the streets of Berlin, London, New York, and Eastern Europe, wearing super-sharp, slim, tailored tuxedo jackets and skinny pants. The monochromatic color palette—usually black—created a base for Slimane's attention to detail and minimalist order. A combination of sheer silk shirts, skinny black ties, and leather or washed denim pants, together with slashed T-shirts, created Slimane's stylized, genderless rock chic.

Slimane's Dior menswear gained international recognition and with it devoted celebrity fans. David Bowie, Brad Pitt, Mick Jagger, and female stars Madonna and Linda Evangelista all have a passion for his sexy and mysterious menswear. Karl Lagerfeld lost weight especially so he could wear nothing but Dior.

In 2007, Hedi Slimane, the architect of Dior's menswear revival, left to pursue other interests. "I love to do projects; I have no intention of ever stopping doing fashion. I really love it. But to always be concentrated on one thing? I'm not sure I want that. I love to create different things," he commented.

Dior Homme for women
Courtney Love is just one of a
long list of women who wear
Hedi Slimane's Dior Homme.

Slimane's creativity is characterized by his love for photography, music, and design. He has published several books, including *London: Birth of a Cult* and *Stage*; designed album covers for Daft Punk; curated exhibitions; exhibited his own work, *Perfect Stranger*, in collaboration with the MUSAC Museum at Galerie Almine Rech in Paris; and designed furniture for Rei Kawakubo's concept store in London's Dover Street Market.

In the late 1980s, Giorgio Armani's influential soft, unstructured silhouette helped to bring about a change in contemporary men's fashion. So far, Hedi Slimane's super-lean rock 'n' roll look has been the modern shape of men's clothing for the new millennium.

His style, besides being spotted in high schools all over the world, has also been imitated by fashion labels such as Pierre Balmain's womenswear line, taking influence from Slimane's Dior Homme glam rock collections.

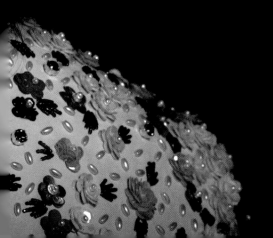

**Dior Homme's Glam Rock
collection, fall/winter 2005/06**
Inspired by glam rockers such as
David Bowie, Hedi's signature
look of a micro tux or
embroidered, sequinned
rock-and-roll-meets-uniform skinny
jacket worn with skinny jeans and
shaggy hair has become a look
copied across the globe.

Zac Posen

"We started with amazing hype from name and personality recognition. It drove this business, and images of celebrities in the clothing drove it."

Zac Posen was brought up in the bohemian SoHo community of New York, among art galleries, boutiques, restaurants, and trendy workspaces. Naturally acquiring a sense for creativity, Posen showed early signs of promise by landing an internship with Nicole Miller and a job as a design assistant with new label Tocca.

In a quest to develop his love for fashion, Posen left New York for London and enrolled onto the highly acclaimed fashion and textiles program at the prestigious Central Saint Martins College of Art and Design. Posen flourished within the creative atmosphere, which placed independent creative vision and integrity at the heart of its academic delivery.

While still a student, Posen exhibited a dress inspired by nineteenth-century underwear at the Curvaceous exhibition held at London's Victoria and Albert Museum (V&A) in 2001–02. Referencing traditional corsetry, he made his dress from several full-length brown leather strips brought together only by hooks and eyes to construct the final outcome. This early rendition of dress exemplified his craftsmanship and conscious approach toward female body contours. The dress is now part of the V&A's permanent collection.

Using a strategy somewhat like that of Paul Poiret, who used the social circuit as a means of promoting his designs in the first decades of the twentieth century, Posen returned to New York and began appearing on the party scene, where models dressed in Zac Posen attire mingled with the socialites who mattered. From the outset, before launching his label, Posen made his fashion intent clear: glamor and celebrity were to be a key part of his vision. He had already acquired a client list that included the likes of Naomi Campbell, Jade Jagger, and Sophie Dahl.

Ready-to-wear collection, spring/summer 2010
Glamorous ball gowns and sexy red-carpet dresses have become Posen's signature look.

catwalk collection at New York Fashion Week in October 2001. Held in high regard by the fashion establishment for his strong design credentials, the following year Posen was the recipient of the Ecco Domani Fashion Foundation award of $25,000. He continued to impress and dress Hollywood heroines with his ultrafeminine silhouettes, which won him the Council of Fashion Designers of America Swarovski Perry Ellis award for Womenswear in 2004. Although the awards and accolades were important in establishing his business, Posen cites the press attention that the awards generated as being more powerful and beneficial.

Referring to A-list actress Natalie Portman as his muse, Zac Posen is able to define his aesthetic; super-streamlined feminine shapes that move with the body in supple shimmering fabrics that lend a modern context to 1940s influences. Hemlines are occasionally embellished with embroidery and graphic prints, which accentuate flared mermaid gowns and cheeky cocktail frocks. These sensuous qualities have enticed the likes of Kate Winslet, Cameron Diaz, Jennifer Lopez, and many other red-carpet stars.

Opposite: Ready-to-wear collection, spring/summer 2010
A pink PVC coat dress worn over a body-hugging digital graphic print dress adds a youthful edge to this collection.

Right: Ready-to-wear collection, spring/summer 2010
Posen's outfit for daywear retains an eye for sophistication and glamor.

Left: Ready-to-wear collection, spring/summer 2010
This powder-blue lasercut suede zipped coat dress with fake fur sleeves is a risqué rock chic statement amid all the sophisticated and glamorous outfits.

Above: Ready-to-wear collection, spring/summer 2010
Posen cuts this deep purple silk dress with the body beautiful in mind; the dress sits close to the body with short proportions. The abstract splash print helps to further highlight the personality of the outfit, which conveys a sexy, carefree attitude.

**Below and center:
Ready-to-wear collection,
fall/winter 2009**
Inspired by the 1940s
silhouette and Victoriana,
Posen creates tailored jackets
with strong shoulders and
nipped-in waists accentuated
by belts. Ruffles on the skirts
soften the overall look.

**Far right: Ready-to-wear
collection, fall/winter 2009**
Posen uses a plunging
neckline, shimmering metallic
jacquard fabric, and a
silhouette cut close to the
body to produce one of his
sexy celebrity dresses.

**Right: Ready-to-wear
collection, spring/summer
2010**
Strong color, print, texture,
and clever draping around the
hips create a silhouette that is
sophisticated while being
young and modern.

Left: Ready-to-wear collection, spring/summer 2010
This tailored suit with green raglan sleeves and off-white sharp triangular side bodice panels creates a graphic, sporty look.

Right: Ready-to-wear collection, spring/summer 2010
A large tiger print designed by artist Rosson Crow looks ready to pounce off Posen's ultra-sexy bias-cut "man-eater" halterneck gown.

Marc Jacobs

"I really think about the clothes and the cut of the clothes, so we try to work the decoration into the seams. We've added borders, piping, and again more top stitching—things that give dimension to otherwise flat fabrics."

Born and bred in New York, Marc Jacobs is a graduate of New York's famous creative hub—Parsons School of Design. He has become America's leading designer and one of the most recognized international fashion brands of the twenty-first century. Jacobs' flourishing career was assured while he was still learning his trade at Parsons. Not only did he design and successfully sell his first collection of handknitted sweaters in New York's reputable boutique Charivari, but he went on to receive numerous awards, including the Perry Ellis Golden Thimble Award, the Chester Weinberg Gold Thimble Award, and the Design Student of the Year Award. This was a sure sign of his talent and his ability to appropriate fashion within a contemporary context.

Upon graduation in 1981, Jacobs was hired at Perry Ellis to work on the womenswear line, which needed new impetus and direction following the death of its founder. Marc Jacobs presented his first collection for Perry Ellis in 1986; it embraced the design philosophy of the house with a touch of his own modern panache. Jacobs won many plaudits, and the following year he presented his own collection under the Marc Jacobs label. Consequently, he became the youngest recipient of the US's highest fashion accolade, the Council of Fashion Designers of America (CFDA) Perry Ellis Award for New Fashion Talent.

Continuing to appropriate modern urban culture in his own unique way, Jacobs' notorious Grunge collection for Perry Ellis in 1992 received lots of press attention for its groundbreaking vision. Influenced by the music and look of the seminal grunge-rock band Nirvana, Jacobs translated ordinary plaid shirts into $1,000 silk shirts impeccably crafted in Italy; interpreted the humble Birkenstock shoe into satin; and transformed the American flag, the epitome of money and power, into cashmere blankets. Jacobs triggered a trend that would be simulated by every segment of the fashion industry. However, his approach was seen as too radical for the Perry Ellis label and he was dismissed from his post. Ironically, Jacobs went on to receive the Womenswear Designer of the Year Award from CFDA the very same year.

Ready-to-wear collection, spring/summer 2010
Suggestive underwear worn over garments asks questions about female power and sexuality.

nfazed by his dismissal and encouraged by s recognition from the CFDA, Jacobs reated collections for the Marc Jacobs bel in the 1990s that reflected the social hood and direction in every way. Inspired by military uniforms and aspects of tailored lhouettes, he created a minimal look uxtaposed with considered elements from nglish Victoriana. His use of color and abric was a clash of classic wools in natural ones demonstrating mature sobriety gainst flashes of bright, youthful color and attern. Once again, the look became a key rend that spread into other market levels.

Culturally tuned in and with an eye for etail, Jacobs is inspired by fashion from revious decades and his personal xperiences of fashion; "I like romantic llusions to the past: what the babysitter vore, what the art teacher wore, what I vore during my experimental days in ashion when I was going to the Mudd Club and wanted to be a New Wave kid or a punk kid but was really a poseur."

Jacobs' wide and varied research allows him to explore the past and translate a modern stylistic vision for the here and now. Not concerned with being conceptual, the Marc Jacobs brand is a business first and foremost, providing the consumer with tasteful contemporary fashion. However, he also believes in taking risks and breaking the mold in order to achieve something new; "I'm most proud of the Perry Ellis collection called Grunge. [It] felt very right; even though it was not what I was supposed to be doing for the image of Perry Ellis, it produced work that has some resonance or

Left: Ready-to-wear collection, spring/summer 2010
Here, Jacobs takes inspiration for make-up and hair from Japanese geishas. A "must-have" accessory–a Marc Jacobs bag–completes the look for the season.

Right: Ready-to-wear collection, spring/summer 2010
A military-inspired six-buttoned double-breasted coat is belted high above the waist to create unconventional proportions that balance out the wide and floaty long skirt.

Right: Ready-to-wear collection, fall/winter 2009
Inspired by the 1980s New York club scene, every aspect of this collection, from crimped hair, "New Romantic" make-up, clothes, proportions, and accessories, is referenced to complete the look.

Opposite (both images): Ready-to-wear collection, fall/winter 2009
Color, expensive luxury fabrics, and bouffant hair help to create a sophisticated interpretation of the 1980s.

Right: Ready-to-wear collection, fall/winter 2009
Pink and green are effectively used as contrast colors, bringing the outfit to life.

Left: Ready-to-wear collection, fall/winter 2009
This shirt takes military details such as color, buttons, and pockets, and is juxtaposed with a luxurious velvet skirt. Black leather gloves, belt, and a quilted pouch complete the look.

Since 1997, alongside designing for his own
label, Marc Jacobs has been the creative
director at Louis Vuitton. He developed the
first ready-to-wear line, which showcases a
distinctly modern vision of referential French
style, and radically redefined the famous
Louis Vuitton bag and monogram. Inspired
by his favorite art piece, Marcel Duchamp's
L.H.O.O.Q.—the defaced *Mona Lisa* bearing
a scribbled-on mustache—Jacobs has been
driven to hipper and more anarchic
interpretations. This has led to creative
collaborations with artists such as Stephen
Sprouse, who created graffiti bags, and
Takashi Murakami, who applied cartoonlike
characters to a colorful LV monogram.
Initially, these new bags, keyrings, and so on
were meant only for fashion shows, but
after the company was inundated with
requests from the public and enthusiastic
press reports, Jacobs finally persuaded the
board to go ahead with production. "Our
collaboration has produced a lot of works,
and has been a huge influence and

inspiration to many. It has been, and continues to be, a monumental marriage of art and commerce. The ultimate crossover —one for both the fashion, and art, history books," he comments.

At the time, Jacobs' appointment to Louis Vuitton was seen as a gamble; his laidback attitude and instinctive zeitgeist qualities seemed to be in stark contrast to a formal and traditional company with a rigid ethos and customer base. However, Jacobs has firmly established the Louis Vuitton brand as a leading luxury fashion house, and he introduced watches and jewelry to expand Vuitton's share of the luxury market.

Jacobs' creative foresight and continuous regurgitation of cool and effortless fashion has served him well, and comparisons with the global queen of luxury fashion, Miuccia Prada, are as frequent as sales of Marc Jacobs handbags. Together with his business partner, right-hand man, and faithful confidante Robert Duffy, Jacobs has built an empire that has numerous standalone stores across the globe, offering products that range from perfume, eyewear and accessories to the most sought-after shoes on the contemporary fashion circuit.

Opposite: Marc Jacobs for Louis Vuitton ready-to-wear collection, fall/winter 2001
Models act as porters to present Louis Vuitton's luggage range. Marc Jacobs in collaboration with Steven Sprouse reworked the traditional LV monogram and changed it into a modern graffiti print.

Left: Marc Jacobs for Louis Vuitton ready-to-wear collection, spring/summer 2007
This chic black outfit is accessorized with a grungy denim patchwork Louis Vuitton bag, adding a street edge to the look. The bag concept was a collaboration between Mark Jacobs and illustrator Julie Verhoeven.

No matter what we design there is a
nsibility that it's totally wearable. It might
t be to everyone's aesthetic, especially
th men, because the roles are so tightly
awn and the lines of what is acceptable
d what is not acceptable are so crazy. The
sence of Duckie Brown is challenging
ose things."

even Cox and Daniel Silver are the pair
hind New York-based menswear label
uckie Brown. Their eclectic mix of classic
iloring and eccentric use of color and
brics has brought about a new modern
enswear perspective that challenges the
ominant conservative and sportswear-
iented US market.

Duckie Brown presented their first
ollection at Gen Art's annual Fresh Faces
part of New York Fashion Week in 2003.
wasn't long before their work caught the
tention of New York's influential fashion
ore Barneys, which gave Duckie Brown
opportunity to sell on their designer floor
ongside established international labels.
ecognizing their ingenuity and individual
pproach, the fashion establishment of New

York nominated the design duo for the
Swarovski Perry Ellis Menswear Award in
2003 and for the Council of Fashion
Designers of America (CFDA) award in 2004
and 2007. The self-funded label is now sold
by several stockists in Japan, London, and
Paris, as well as across the US.

The pair came together to form Duckie
Brown in 2001. Stephen Cox, the English
lead designer, trained in Britain and spent
more than fifteen years in New York
designing for various labels including Ralph
Lauren and Tommy Hilfiger. Daniel Silver
comes from Toronto, Canada. His first
experience of design was as a glove
designer in the 1980s. He later spent
several successful years as a television
producer. As well as contributing to the
creative discussion, Silver oversees the
business side of the label.

The somewhat diverse backgrounds
of the two men, and their rich mix of
experiences, have come to emphasize
the character of their menswear fashion.
The name Duckie Brown is a throwback to
Cox's childhood, when his aunt called him
"Duckie." The pair added "Brown" because
it's a very classic English surname.

Spring/summer 2008
A silk satin tailored jacket
and a low-cut shirt in a style
more usually associated with
womenswear add feminine
qualities to a masculine
silhouette.

This highlights the label's design intent—a quirky twist on classic menswear based on key English tailored garments that include suits, tailored jackets, and pants.

However, the Duckie Brown aesthetic goes further than just a spin on classic tailoring. Cox is inspired by all aspects of British culture; Silver by personal experiences and music. Above all, both constantly pursue originality through their fashion interpretations. They cite the likes of Rei Kawakubo, Ralph Lauren, Karl Lagerfeld, and Dries Van Noten as mentors.

By infusing an array of different fabric combinations and colors, which sometimes include unusual surface embellishments such as appliqué and beading, they juxtapose playful oversized proportions with shirts and knitwear, all housed within a constrained archetypal silhouette. Their collections cleverly subvert the notion of traditional classical menswear with an underlying sense of humor. Accessories such as underpants with attached gloves or a Scottish man's kilt that is more like a cummerbund are comical almost to the point of absurdity.

Describing themselves as a relatively small company, the duo are passionate about keeping the Duckie Brown label independent, both financially and creatively. They keep their production based in New York, thereby maintaining control of the process from start to finish. By using New York's last remaining Italian handmade tailoring company, they ensure that they obtain the high-end design, quality, and finish they strive for.

Cox and Silver's careful blend of commercialism and creativity has enabled Duckie Brown to grow from strength to strength. Alongside a loyal band of fashion lovers, their aesthetic and fashion-forward menswear vision is now attracting a more discerning male consumer. A notable collaboration with the century-old American footwear brand Florsheim in 2009 further highlights Duckie Brown's design credentials and appreciation for design authenticity, tradition, and quality.

Far left: Spring/summer 2008
Luxurious gold velvet transforms this oversized urban sweat top into casual chic.

Left: Fall/winter 2007
Traditional British elements are apparent in this Scottish tartan-inspired double-breasted tailored jacket, which is beautifully crafted using time-honored techniques. The meticulous matching of the checks is a skill employed by the renowned Savile Row tailors of London.

Left: Spring/summer 2007
The designers subvert the
traditional male suit by
playing with oversized
proportions, sportswear
details, and layering the
vest over the jacket.

Right: Spring/summer 2007
This everyday man's white shirt is oversized and lengthened, creating a lean contemporary silhouette.

Right and center:
Fall/winter 2007
Opposite far right: Spring/
summer 2008
In all three of these outfits,
a splash of color drastically
transforms the persona of
rather mundane garments into
modern menswear fashion
statements.

Right: Fall/winter 2004
Tradition and humor play key
roles in directing Duckie
Brown's design aesthetic.

Opposite: Fall/winter 2004
A Scottish kilt is drastically
shortened, becoming a
comical statement rather than
a literal cultural reference.

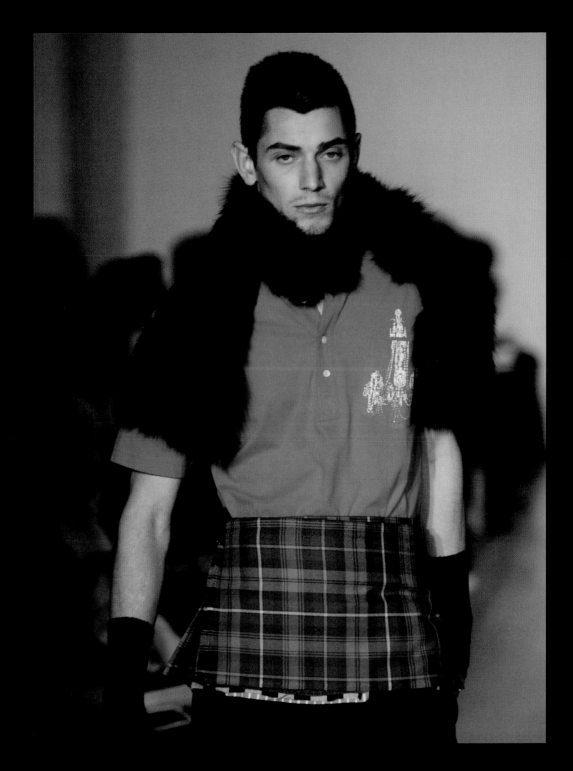

Rick Owens

"My main concept is that you don't have to be so conceptual. I'm minimal and straightforward."

Known for his inspired rock gothic chic look, with a careful blend of grunge and glamor, Rick Owens has become one of the hottest international fashion labels around. Winning the Council of Fashion Designers of America (CFDA) Perry Ellis Award for Emerging Talent in 2002 proved to be a significant launchpad for his career. An Italian company was soon on board to take care of his production, and, if all this weren't enough, his love for designing with fur caught the attention of the luxury French furrier Revillon, which appointed him as creative director. Moving his design studio and home from Los Angeles to Paris was the next logical step. He now has flagship stores in Paris, London, New York, and Tokyo, as well as numerous stockists around the world.

Owens' success is a far cry from his somewhat humble beginnings. A dropout fine-art student, he enrolled onto a pattern-cutting course at an LA trade college, where he made a name for himself as a highly creative and accomplished pattern-cutter.

Overleaf: Ready-to-wear collection, fall/winter 2007/08
This collection takes on a mysterious medieval theme. Volume, texture, and shapes are inspired by caricatures portraying the women of Paul Poiret (the early twentieth-century Parisian couturier) as insects, as drawn by French cartoonist Sem.

Right: Ready-to-wear collection, spring/summer 2007
Models wait backstage ready to walk onto the catwalk. The designer and his team will have spent several days matching models to specific outfits and then planning the running order accordingly.

Owens' first taste of fashion was far from being original or glamorous. He worked for a small back-street company in the LA garment district, knocking off patterns from designer clothes such as Versace. Owens recalls; "it was the most amazing training. It made you really accurate and really fast."

His unassuming fashion apprenticeship continued; he worked for several sportswear companies before embarking on a career as an independent designer. In 1994, Owens set up base in LA and launched his own label, selling his collections to established LA boutiques such as Charles Gallay. It wasn't too long before his work was recognized and his reputation grew.

At ease with both womenswear and menswear, Owens' vision for both has a similar character and aesthetic. He makes no claims to be a super-conceptual designer who is trying to impress the fashion media. He is more intent on commercial success and volume sales, concentrating on delivering tasteful separates and everyday basic classics that flatter his customers. In his own words, "I'm just a wannabe Calvin Klein or Giorgio Armani."

Alongside his essentials, Owens offers clothes inspired by the gloomy, tortured, and distorted paintings of British artist Francis Bacon. The garments are beautifully cut and engineered, incorporating the intricate techniques of the 1930s and 40s. There are bias-cut dresses, sculpted and semisculpted outfits, and alluring fur coats with an urban twist, all in a palette of haunting dark colors with a splash of tonal beiges. His fitted, cropped, distressed leather jackets with asymmetric zips and contour cutting take reference from the rebel biker jacket. These jackets have become a regular feature in his collections, and have become a classic in their own right.

Owens' menswear is similarly inspired by darkness and grunge. Traditional menswear pieces and attributes take on hard, repetitive lines inspired by the war bunkers of western France. The Rick Owens downbeat, minimal, rock classic lived-in look provides the male wearer with an attitude of anti-glamor chic.

Rick Owens presents both womenswear and menswear collections at Paris Fashion Week on a regular basis.

Ready-to-wear collection, spring/summer 2007
Inspired by childhood memories of images of mysterious intergalactic queens, as seen in the fantasy illustrations of Frank Frazetta, Owens presents a collection of organdie and leather asymmetric jackets crunched up around the neck, paired with complex draped skirts.

**Above: Ready-to-wear
collection, spring/summer
2010**
Owens presents asymmetric
and geometrically angled
leather biker jackets, stiff
papery apron tunics,
bodysuits, and sheer
one-shoulder tops, features
that have become key parts
of his design aesthetic.

**Above: Menswear
collection, fall/winter
2009/10**
Owens' successful menswear
line shows the same urban
grunge and gothic design
aesthetic as appears in his
ready-to-wear womenswear.

Ready-to-wear collection, spring/summer 2009
This collection is appropriately titled "Priestesses of Longing." The headpieces, which resemble nuns' wimples, are transformed into contemporary fashion statements, while the garments have an old-school couture elegance.

Left: Palais Royal fur line, spring/summer 2010
Regarded as a master of contemporary fur design, Rick Owens launched his Palais Royal line, exclusively made from fur and leather, in 2008.

Right: Ready-to-wear collection, fall/winter 2009/10
Backstage, a dresser makes last-minute checks, ensuring that the models and garments look perfect before they step out in front of international buyers and the fashion press.

Left: Ready-to-wear collection, fall/winter 2009/10
Here, severe molded shoulders, high wrapped necks, and sharp asymmetric cutaway center fronts are juxtaposed with semi-fluted A-line back panels that soften a strong utilitarian look.

Overleaf: Ready-to-wear collection, spring/summer 2010
Adding to the asymmetric and geometric silhouettes, models wear futuristic angled space-warrior bracelets, which complete the look for the season.

"New York has always inspired my work. It's an incredible melting pot of different cultures; it is the crossroads of American, European, Asian, and Far Eastern communities. It has always had a position where everything enters here, and ideas mix."

American sportswear has a great tradition built on ingenuity and realistic lifestyle applications. In the same mold as sportswear designers of yesteryear, such as Claire McCardell and Geoffrey Beene, Derek Lam retains the enthusiasm to innovate and create an informal elegance between sportswear and ready-to-wear.

Born into the clothing industry, from a young age Lam experienced the process of garment production at his family's wedding dress atelier in San Francisco. He was fascinated by the beauty of cloth and admired the skilful techniques used to transform pieces of cut fabric into beautiful designs. In pursuit of a career in contemporary fashion, Lam moved from San Francisco to New York to study fashion design at Parsons School of Design. Upon his graduation in 1990, Lam secured a job with the established sportswear and ready-to-wear designer Michael Kors. Having spent the best part of ten years with Kors assisting and heading up the design direction, Lam launched his own label in 2003.

Lam's invaluable insight into American classics and the, at times intense, experience of Michael Kors' mentorship helped him to develop his own aesthetic vision for sportswear chic. Lam presented his debut collection in September 2003 during New York Fashion Week for spring/summer 2004, and the fashion press declared the collection a success. The major fashion retailers Barneys and Bergdorf Goodman followed up with orders for his eclectic mix of classy and casual chic.

Born out of the legacy of American sportswear elegance, Lam's subsequent collections continue to engage with his core aesthetic, assembling everyday separates such as shirts, cardigans, and skirts into coordinated contemporary daywear and stylish eveningwear looks. Signature looks combine luxurious wools, silks, and cashmeres, occasionally juxtaposed with Chinese-influenced fabrics.

Somewhat akin to Eileen Gray's architecture, his silhouettes are modern, with crisp, clean lines and finely worked details such as embroidery, pintucking, lace inserts, and pleating that flatters and moves with the body. These key ingredients enable Lam's clothes to become sophisticated, wearable timeless classics. "I am interested in what it means to live a contemporary life," says Lam. "I always consider what will work for women at this moment, and to me this moment is about luxury without formality."

Ready-to-wear collection, fall/winter 2008/09
Contrasting black satin neck and waist details cleverly frame and define body proportions for this long, purple organza dress.

Winner of many fashion accolades, including the Ecco Domani Fashion Foundation Award in 2004, the Council of Fashion Designers of America (CFDA)'s Swarovski Perry Ellis Award for Emerging Talent in 2005, and CFDA's Accessory Designer of the Year Award in 2007, Derek Lam continues to cement his creative reputation within American contemporary fashion. As well as designing his own ready-to-wear, resort, shoes, bags, and jewelry lines, which have more than 120 stockists around the world, Lam also takes charge of all creative operations for the Italian luxury house Tod's. He was appointed creative director in 2006 to oversee their ready-to-wear range as well as developing their shoe and bag ranges.

Right: Ready-to-wear collection, fall/winter 2008/09
Inspired by his theme of "Controlled Exuberance," Lam presents a sleeveless tailored jacket with a fur collar. The tailoring indicates "control," while the fur and the sleeveless elements reference "exuberance."

Far right: Ready-to-wear collection, fall/winter 2008/09
This gold lace dress exhibits the oriental qualities often seen in Lam's work.

Ready-to-wear collection, fall/winter 2009/10
This halterneck dress in silk georgette is cut with drapes and folds to reveal the sensuousness of the female body, thereby creating a romantic mood resembling Pre-Raphaelite paintings.

Far left: Ready-to-wear collection, fall/winter 2009/10
Inspired by the colors and textures of Yves Saint Laurent's interiors and Louis Malle's 1958 movie *Ascenseur pour l'échafaud*, starring Jeanne Moreau as a wicked film noir heroine, Lam presents a dramatic coyote fur coat with a beige and gray jacquard dress.

Left: Ready-to-wear collection, fall/winter 2009/10
This taupe-colored, body-hugging jersey dress is cut on the bias, which enables the designer to create beautiful sweeping Grecian-like drapes.

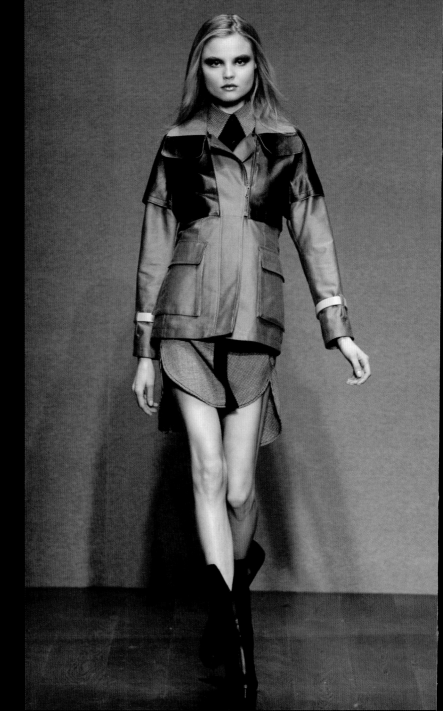

**Ready-to-wear collection,
fall/winter 2010/11**
Black and tan leather are
worked together to create an
interesting trompe l'oeil effect.
Teamed with a shirtdress,
the outfit becomes young
and sexy while retaining an
urban look.

Far left: Ready-to-wear collection, fall/winter 2010/11
The legendary cowboy of the American Wild West is an important reference for this collection. This strict tailored caramel moleskin coat with black vintage leather sleeves has a contemporary slim silhouette. Milliner Albertus Swanepoel designed the cowboy hat.

Left: Ready-to-wear collection, fall/winter 2010/11
Gray speckled tweed bodice panels and a long sweeping scarf help soften a strong leather-dominated outfit.

Right: Ready-to-wear collection, fall/winter 2010/11
Floor-length, flared silk gazar trousers teamed with a shrunken marled wool sweater create an illusion of long legs.

Far right: Ready-to-wear collection, fall/winter 2010/11
Lam converts the urban sports blouson jacket into a luxury chic garment by simply changing the fabric from predictable nylon to opulent fur.

Glossary

Abstract
A concept or idea that depicts a detached reality.

Aesthetic
In a fashion context, a set of principles that relate to the sensitive translation of fabric, cut, scale, color, texture, research references, and style.

Appliqué
A decorative patch or purposely-shaped piece of fabric sewn onto a base fabric.

Asymmetrical
Uneven or unequal sides or parts of a garment.

Atelier
A French term used to describe a workroom or studio used by an artist, designer, or couturier.

Balance
i) The correct hang of a garment at the front, back, and sides.
ii) Pleasing proportions of the components that make up the overall design.

Basic pattern block
A basic 2D pattern template of a garment, for example a dress, that is used as a starting point and then adapted to draft a pattern according to the design.

Bespoke
A term to describe a garment that has been made specifically according to the customer's personal measurements, a practice that is particularly used in men's tailoring.

Bias cut
To cut a woven fabric on the cross or at 45 degrees to the vertical selvedge. This cutting technique is used to make woven fabric more fluid and elastic.

Bodice
The upper part of the body or garment, excluding arms or sleeves.

Brief
Outlines a set of instructions to be carried out by the designer in order to complete a task or collection.

Calico
i) In North America, calico is used to describe inexpensive cotton fabrics, printed with allover patterns.
ii) In the UK, calico refers to a type of cheap fabric used for making prototypes. See also muslin.

Catwalk show
A parade of garments on live models in front of press and buyers. Also known as a "runway show."

Chambre Syndicale De Le Couture Parisienne
A body that regulates, approves, and oversees the running of the haute couture industry in France.

Classic garment
A garment that stands the test of time and never goes out of style, such as the little black dress.

Collection
A group of garments designed specifically with common attributes, such as color, silhouettes, and details.

Color palette
A group of colors that have been brought together by the designer to form the color story for a collection.

Colorways
Either singular colors or groups of colors that offer alternative options in prints or garments.

Contoured garment
A garment that follows the natural outer lines of the body.

Couturier
A person who designs haute couture fashion.

Crinoline
A stiff underskirt made of horsehair and cotton or linen used in the 1800s and early 1900s to support the exaggerated silhouettes of skirts.

Concept
An artistic vision based on ideas and principles with deep intellectualization

Contemporary
Current, modern, and stylish fashion, design, or art.

Costing
Working out the cost of producing a garment or collection. Includes elements such as cost of fabrics, production, labor, overheads, etc.

Dart
Excess fabric folded and stitched down, tapering at one end or both ends, which creates shape on a garment allowing it to fit the body. Darts are commonly employed around the bust area, which are known as bust darts.

Drape
i) Term used to describe the way fabric falls.
ii) A technique of hanging fabric to create folds in order to cover the body or mannequin in an elegant way.

Drops
Staggered introduction of collections and ranges throughout a season. This commercial tactic is used mainly in the mass market.

Embroidery
Decorative stitching made either by hand or machine.

Fastenings
Items used to keep a garment closed, such as zippers, buttons, hooks and eyes, Velcro, etc.

Fitting
A session to adjust a garment according to the design and sizing requirements. This is usually done on a model or the client.

Flats
Drawings that form the technical blueprint of a garment. Flats show front and back views, styled details, stitch details, measurements, etc. Also known as spec drawings.

Forecasting
The process of predicting forthcoming trends.

Freelance designer
A fashion designer who is self-employed and able to work for a number of different companies, rather than being committed to just one.

Haute couture
French term that literally means "high dressmaking." Haute couture is made to order specifically for individual clients, and involves the use of the highest quality of fabrics, techniques, and procedures.

High street fashion
Term used in the UK for mass-market, ready-to-wear clothes, sold through chain stores.

Journal
i) A dedicated magazine or newspaper published to report the latest news of a specialist subject, for example *Drapers* reports the latest news in the fashion industry.
ii) Another word to describe a sketchbook.

Juxtapose
To put different elements together in order to emphasize a complete contrast between them.

Lay or lay plan
A method used whereby pattern pieces are laid out on the fabric in the most economical way. Mass-production sectors use computer aided technology to do this, using Lectra or Gerber software.

Look book
A catalog of styled and photographed "looks" used to present a season's collection to the press and buyers.

Line up
Edited collection showing the complete essence of a range. The line up can be either presented illustratively or in 3D form.

Mannequin
Also know as a dummy or a dressmaking stand. It replicates the human body and comes in different sizes and body shapes. A mannequin is used in place of a live model.

Mood board
Compilation of research, images, colors, fabrics, and key inspirational words composed together to communicate and present a theme or design idea. Also sometimes referred to as a "storyboard."

Muse
A real or imaginary person who is inspirational to the designer, helping him or her to create a distinctive look.

Muslin
Unbleached, cheap cotton used for making toiles or prototypes, which is available in different weights. In the UK, this fabric is known as calico.

Pantone color system
Internationally recognized colors and shades, each with an individual number. They are used throughout the creative industries.

Portfolio
A presentation folder in which the contents show the designer's work and represent his or her aesthetic.

Prêt-a-porter
French term that means "ready-to-wear."

Production pattern
A pattern that has been corrected and finalized, marked with special instructions, and made out of card, ready to be used in manufacturing.

Ready-to-wear
Provides high fashion, style, design, concept, and quality off the peg. Garments are not made to measure.

Season
In fashion terms, this describes the seasons associated with the fashion collections and fashion shows: Spring/Summer and Fall/Winter.

Selvedge
The finished woven edge of a fabric.

Silhouette
The outline shape of a garment or outfit.

Stand work
A term to describe 3D design work or experiments carried out on a mannequin.

Swatch
A small cut piece of fabric used as a reference and example of the fabric's color, texture, and weight.

Tear sheet
An inspirational page, cut or torn out from a magazine to be used in a sketchbook or on a mood board.

Toile
The first 3D trial or "mock up" of a garment made in muslin to test the pattern, style, and fit before it is finalized and made in the real fabric.

Trend scout
A person employed to search for new trends.

Zeitgeist
A German expression that means "spirit of the times." The term is used in relation to seeking new trends and trend forecasting.

Resources

Books

70s Style and Design. Dominic Lutyens & Kirsty Hislop. Thames & Hudson, 2009.

The Art of Fashion Draping. Connie Amaden-Crawford. Fairchild Publications, 2005.

Balenciaga. Lesley Ellis Miller. V&A Publications, 2007.

Belgian Fashion Design. Luc Derycke, Sandra Van De Veire, Flanders Fashion Institute. Ludion Editions, 1999.

Classic Tailoring Techniques: A Construction Guide for Men's Wear. Roberto Cabrera & Patricia Flaherty Meyers. Fairchild Publications, 1983.

Classic Tailoring Techniques: A Construction Guide for Women's Wear. Roberto Cabrera & Patricia Flaherty Meyers. Fairchild Publications, 1984.

Costume and Fashion. Bronwyn Cosgrave. Hamlyn, 2003.

Decades of Beauty: The Changing Images of Women 1890s–1990s. Kate Mulvey & Melissa Richards. Hamlyn, 1998.

Decades of Fashion. Harriet Worsley. Könemann, 2000.

Dior by Dior: The Autobiography of Christian Dior. V&A Publications, 2007.

Dress in Detail: From Around the World. Rosemary Crill, Jennifer Wearden, Verity Wilson. V&A Publications, 2002.

Extreme Beauty: The Body Transformed. Harold Koda. Yale University Press, 2001.

Fashion. Christopher Breward. OUP, 2003.

Fashion: The Collection of the Kyoto Costume Institute—A History from the 18th to the 20th Century. Akiko Fukai (Ed.). Taschen, 2002.

Fashion as Communication (Second Edition). Malcolm Barnard. Routledge, 2002.

Fashion Marketing: Contemporary Issues. Tony Hines & Margaret Bruce. Butterworth-Heinemann, 2004

Fashion Source Book. Kathryn McKelvey. Wiley Blackwell, 2006.

Fashion Statements: Interviews with Fashion Designers. Francesca Alfano Miglietti. Skira Editore, 2006.

Historical Fashion in Detail: The 17th and 18th Centuries. Avril Hart & Susan North. V&A Publications, 1998.

History of 20th Century Fashion. Elizabeth Ewing & Alice Mackrell. Batsford, 2001.

Madeleine Vionnet. Betty Kirke. Chronicle Books, 1997.

Metric Pattern Cutting. Winifred Aldrich. WileyBlackwell, 2004.

Modern Menswear. Hywel Davies. Laurence King, 2008.

The New English Dandy. Alice Cicolini. Thames & Hudson, 2007.

Nineteenth Century Fashion in Detail. Lucy Johnston. V&A Publications, 2005.

People in Vogue: A Century of Portrait Photography. Robin Derrick & Robin Muir (Eds.). Little, Brown, 2005.

The Power of Fashion: About Design and Meaning. Jan Brand, Jose Teunissen, Anne Van Der Zwaag (Eds.). Terra Uitgeverij, 2006.

Professional Fashion Illustration. Julian Seaman. Batsford Ltd., 1995.

Radical Fashion. Claire Wilcox (Ed.). V&A Publications, 2001.

Shocking Life: The Autobiography of Elsa Schiaparelli. Elsa Schiaparelli. V&A Publications, 2007.

Skin + Bones: Parallel Practices in Fashion and Architecture. Brooke Hodge, Patricia Mears, Susan Sidlauskas. Thames & Hudson, 2006.

Street: The Nylon Book of Global Style. Marvin Scott Jarrett. Universe Publishing, 2006.

Tim Walker Pictures. Tim Walker. TeNeues, 2008.

Unseen Vogue: The Secret History of Fashion Photography. Robin Derrick & Robin Muir (Eds.). Little, Brown, 2004.

Visionaries: Interviews with Fashion Designers. Susannah Frankel. V&A Publications, 2001.

Woman in the Mirror: 1945–2004. Richard Avedon & Anne Hollander. Abrams, 2005.

Museums and Costume Galleries

Brooklyn Museum
200 Eastern Parkway
Brooklyn
NY 11238
USA
www.brooklynmuseum.org

Centro Internazionale Arti e del Costume
Palazzo Grassi
S.Samuele 3231
20124 Venice
Italy

Costume Gallery
Los Angeles County Museum of Art
5905 Wilshire Boulevard
Los Angeles
CA 90036
USA
www.lacma.org

Costume Institute
Metropolitan Museum of Art
1000 5th Avenue at 82nd Street
New York
NY 10028-0198
USA
www.metmuseum.org

Fashion Museum
Assembly Rooms
Bennett Street
Bath
BA1 2HQ
UK
www.museumofcostume.co.uk

Kobe Fashion Museum
Rokko Island
Kobe
Japan
www.fashionmuseum.or.jp

Kostum Forschungsinstitut
Kemnatenstrasse 50
8 Munich 19
Germany

MoMu
Nationalestraat 28
B – 2000 Antwerp
Belgium
www.momu.be

Musée de la Mode et du Costume
10 Avenue Pierre 1er de Serbie
75016 Paris
France
www.ucad.fr

Musée de la Mode et textile
Palais du Louvre
107 rue de Rivoli
75001 Paris
France
www.ucad.fr

Le musée des Tissus et des Arts Décoratifs
34 rue de la Charité
F-69002 Lyon
France
www.musee-des-tissus.com

Museum at the Fashion Institute of Technology
7th Avenue at 27th Street
New York
NY 10001-5992
USA
www.fitnyc.edu

Museum Salvatore Ferragamo
Palazzo Spini Feroni
Via Tornabuoni 2
Florence 50123
Italy

Victoria and Albert Museum (V&A)
Cromwell Road
South Kensington
London
SW7 2RL
UK
www.vam.ac.uk

Wien Museum
(Fashion collection with public library)
A-1120 Vienna
Hetzendorfer
Strasse 79
Austria

Useful Websites

www.style.com

www.infomat.com

www.showstudio.com

International Fashion Weeks:

Australia

Australian Fashion Week
www.rafw.com.au

Europe

Milan
www.cameramoda.it

Paris
www.modeaparis.com

UK

British Fashion Council
www.londonfashionweek.co.uk

USA

Council of Fashion Designers of America
www.cfda.com

New York Fashion Week
www.mbfashionweek.com

Trade Shows

Pitti Filati
www.pittimmagine.com

Première Vision
www.premierevision.fr

Rendez-Vous Paris
www.rendez-vous-paris.com

Tissu Premier
www.tissu-premier.com

Trend Forecasting

www.carlininternational.com

www.fashioninformation.com

www.kjaer-global.com

www.promostyl.com

www.stylesignal.com

www.thefuturelaboratory.com

www.trendstop.com

www.wgsn-edu.com

Magazines

10 Magazine (UK)

A Magazine (Belgium)

Another Magazine (UK)

Arena Homme + (UK)

Collezioni Uomo (Italy)

Citizen K (France)

Dansk (Denmark)

Dazed & Confused (UK, Japan, Korea)

Elle (published internationally)

Fantastic Man (Netherlands & UK)

Flux (UK)

Fudge (Japan)

Ginza (Japan)

Glamour (published internationally)

GQ (USA & UK)

Grazia (published internationally)

Harper's Bazaar (USA & UK)

i-D magazine (UK)

InStyle (USA & UK)

Marie Claire (published internationally)

Numéro Magazine (France)

Nylon (USA)

Vogue (published internationally)

Pop (UK)

Purple (France)

S Magazine (Denmark)

Self Service (France)

Selvedge (UK)

Seventeen (USA)

Surface (USA)

Tank (UK)

V Magazine (USA)

Velvet (Greece)

Visionaire (USA)

VS (published internationally)

Women's Wear Daily (WWD) (USA)

Index

Adidas 73–74
Aestheticterrorists 166
Alaïa, Azzedine 25, 33
American Express 142
Amies, Hardy 25
Amsterdam 134
androgyny 8–9, 24, 148, 174
animal skins 8
anorexia 60
Antwerp 35, 160, 169
Armani, Giorgio 49, 54–55,
    61–62, 67, 70, 75, 178,
    220
Arnault, Bernard 34, 48
art 11–15, 74, 79, 81, 84, 98,
    122, 148, 205
art deco 21
arthouse films 38
Arts and Crafts movement 11
Atomic Bomb 137
awards 81, 123, 174, 184,
    192, 194, 206, 216, 234

Bacon, Francis 220
balance 27, 104–5, 110, 117
Balenciaga, Cristobal 25, 27,
    30–32, 47
Balmain, Pierre 178
Bartley, Luella 126
Bedtime Story 138
Beene, Geoffrey 232
Bells 137
Berge, Pierre 172
Berlin 25, 177
bias cut 24–25, 104, 220
Bikkembergs, Dirk 35, 160
Birtwell, Celia 30
Black Hole 138
Black Light 137
Blahnik, Manolo 54
Blass, Bill 30
Bless 169
blueprints 115
BMI (body mass index) 61
Boateng, Ozwald 75
body image 58, 60–61, 151
body painting 8
body piercing 8, 32
Bottega Veneta 47
Boudicca 67, 140–47
Bourdin, Guy 40
Bow, Clara 52
Bowie, David 9, 177
Boy George 9
brailing 81
Broach, Zowie 140
Brummell, Beau 75
bubble-up effect 79
Bump 151
Burberry 54, 73

calendar 86–93
Canino, Patricia 38
Cardin, Pierre 30, 48

careers 118–27
Carnaby Street 30
catwalk shows 6, 18, 30, 55,
    58, 60–62, 76–77, 84,
    86–87, 102, 184
Cavalli, Roberto 50, 62
celebrities 32, 39, 52–57, 61,
    85, 182
Celine 34, 46
Chalayan, Hussein 74
Chambre Syndicale de la
    Couture Parisienne 21, 25,
    66–67, 80, 92, 135, 142
Chanel, Gabrielle (Coco) 12,
    22–24, 32–33, 38, 48,
    54, 72, 78, 92, 118, 148
Chanel No 5 22
Chester Weinberg Gold
    Thimble Award 192
Le Chevalie, Jérome 172
Chloé 32, 34, 47
Choo, Jimmy 50, 54
cinema see movies
Clark, Ossie 30, 32
climate change 64
clothing definition 6
collaborations 18, 38, 40,
    50–51, 56–57, 73–74, 76,
    93, 98, 138, 142, 152,
    163, 169, 178, 203, 209
colleges 118–21, 124, 172
Colonna, Jean 130
color 6, 8, 11–12, 15, 30,
    32, 35, 40, 54, 69, 75,
    78–81, 83, 88, 91, 96,
    99–100, 104, 106–10,
    112, 114, 120, 122,
    124–25, 135, 148, 163,
    177, 194, 206, 209
Comme des Garçons 50, 70,
    75, 78, 130, 148–59
competitions 122, 124
context 15, 38, 98, 119,
    121–22, 148, 184
cool hunters 81–82
corsets 21, 24, 27, 78
Council of Fashion Designers
    of America (CFDA) 174,
    184, 192, 194, 206,
    216, 234
Courreges, André 30
courses 118–23
Cox, Steven 206, 209
Creed 27
Cubism 11
culture 6, 8, 15, 18, 30,
    38, 40, 49, 64, 70, 72,
    74, 78–79, 81, 93, 98,
    122, 194
cycles 88–89

Daan, Wendelien 134
Dalí, Salvador 12
De La Renta, Oscar 30

Deacon, Giles 51
Dean, James 38
degrees 118–19, 124
Delaunay, Sonia 11
Demeulemeester, Ann 35,
    107, 152, 160
democratization 48–51
demographics 81
design process 96–117
Design Student of the Year
    Award 192
diffusion lines 49–50, 70, 76
Dior, Christian 27–28, 46–47,
    49, 67, 78, 85, 98, 103,
    126, 148, 172, 174,
    177–78
Doherty, Pete 174
Dolce & Gabbana 49, 55, 70
dolls 134
drawing skills 101–2, 105, 120
Duchamp, Marcel 203
Duckie Brown 206–15
Duffy, Robert 205
DuPont 32

eating disorders 60
Ecco Domani Fashion
    Foundation 184, 234
ecology 58, 62, 64, 166
economics 6, 28, 32, 34,
    39, 44, 47–48, 50, 62,
    64, 67, 70, 92
editors 32, 38–39, 42, 55, 85
Empire (Directoire) Line 21
endorsements 54–55
England, Katy 84
Estethica 65
ethics 58–65
exhibitions 15, 38, 83, 130,
    137, 140, 142, 169, 172,
    178, 182

fabric 6, 11, 21–22, 24–25,
    28, 30, 32, 40, 44, 64,
    72–73, 75, 78–81, 83, 88,
    91, 96–97, 99–100, 104,
    106–7, 109–10, 112, 114,
    116–17, 122, 124–25,
    130, 135, 148, 163, 184,
    194, 206, 209, 232
Facebook 124
fair trade 65
fall/winter collections 6, 66,
    70, 86–87, 90–92, 109,
    137–38, 142
The Fashion Show 138
fashion weeks 61, 65, 70,
    86–93, 137, 140, 166,
    184, 206, 220, 232
fast fashion 64, 76, 92
feathers 8
Fendi 46
Festival International de Mode
    et de Photographie 130

Field, Patricia 84
Figgis, Mike 142
final-year projects 112, 122
finance 126, 137
first-year projects 122
Flappers 24, 103
Florsheim 209
Flowerbomb 138
Ford, Tom 34, 47
forecasting 80–82
Forever-A Dream Sequence
    142
Fortuny, Mariano 22
freelance work 125
Fresh Faces 184, 206
fur 58, 62, 216, 220

Galliano, John 25, 34, 47, 49,
    96, 123, 126
Ganryu 152
La Garçonne 24
Gen Art 184, 206
Gibb, Bill 30
Gilbert and George 130
Givenchy, Hubert de 28, 34,
    38, 46–47, 99, 112, 126
graduates 112, 119, 124–25,
    148, 160
graduation collections 122
Grand, Katie 84
Gray, Eileen 232
grunge 34, 75, 78, 148, 192,
    194, 216, 220
Gucci 34, 42, 47, 74, 174

H&M 50, 54, 56, 76, 138, 152
hair 6, 8, 24, 30, 32, 93, 115
Halston 30
handbags 32, 44, 49, 84, 205
haute couture 21, 25, 28, 30,
    34–35, 40, 44, 46–48,
    66–67, 69–70, 80–81, 83,
    86–87, 92, 96, 135, 137,
    142, 144, 148
headhunting 124
hemlines 22, 24, 35, 80,
    110, 184
Hepburn, Audrey 28, 38, 99
Hermès 34, 47
Highland Rape 34
Hilfiger, Tommy 206
hippies 30, 32, 34
Hiroshima Chic 148
history 6, 9, 97–98, 122,
    135, 205
Hollywood 25, 28, 33,
    54–56, 62, 184
Horsting, Viktor 130

identity 6, 8–9, 28, 34, 38,
    40, 47, 72, 84, 112, 124
illustrations 115
independent labels 40, 90,
    92, 112, 125–26

internet 42, 44, 78, 97, 118, 124, 163
internships 122, 125, 182
interviews 121, 124
investors 126

Jacobs, Marc 34, 49, 62, 123, 192–205
James, Richard 75
jobs 127

Karan, Donna 34, 46, 49
Kawakubo, Rei 33, 78, 118, 148–59, 178, 209
Kelly, Grace 28
Kenzo 46
Kings Road 30
Kirkby, Brian 140
Klein, Calvin 27, 34, 49, 70, 84, 112, 220
Knight, Nick 40
Kokosalaki, Sophia 103
Kors, Michael 34, 232
Kurihara, Tao 152

Labour Behind the Label 64
Lagerfeld, Karl 32–33, 48, 50, 172, 177, 209
Lam, Derek 232–45
Lang, Helmut 47, 84
Launch 134–35
Lauren, Ralph 34, 70, 92, 118, 206, 209
lead times 90
Left Bank 172
Lennox, Annie 9
Lévy, José 172
Lichtenstein, Roy 15
Lindbergh, Peter 61
line 27, 104–5, 110, 117, 124
little black dress 24, 32–33, 92
London 21, 30, 32, 34, 48–49, 65, 67, 70, 72, 75, 86–87, 93, 140, 144, 152, 160, 166, 177–78, 182, 206, 216
Long Live the Immaterial 138
Los Angeles 72, 216, 220
Lucile 38
luxury brands 46–51, 62
LVMH 34, 46–49, 67, 174
Lycra 33

Mabille, Alexis 67
McCardell, Claire 27, 72, 232
McCartney, Stella 34, 47, 50, 62, 74, 123
MacDonald, Julien 34
McLaren, Malcolm 32
McQueen, Alexander 34, 38, 47, 51, 54, 74, 84, 104, 123, 126, 142
Madrid 61

magazines 18, 39, 53, 56, 58, 60–61, 78–79, 81–82, 84, 97, 107, 128, 134, 169, 253
make-up 6, 28, 35, 40, 93, 115
Margiela, Martin 34, 75, 79, 103, 105, 130, 152, 160
Marks & Spencer 76
mass-market fashion 50, 70, 76–77, 90, 96, 126
media 6
menswear 72–73, 75, 78, 86–87, 122, 138, 148, 160, 166, 172, 174, 177, 206, 209, 220
Milan 61, 70, 75, 86–87, 93, 138
Miller, Nicole 182
mini skirt 30
miniature collections 134
Minney, Safia 65
Miu Miu 49, 84
Miyake, Issey 34
models 30, 32, 56, 60–62, 117, 135, 172, 182
Moet Hennessy 46
Molyneux, Edward 27
Mondrian, Piet 15
Monsieur 138
Montana, Claude 32–33
mood boards 100, 114
Morton, Digby 25
Mosca, Bianca 27
Moss, Kate 34, 54, 56–57, 84
movies 6, 12, 28, 38, 81, 142, 169
Mugler, Thierry 33
Mumbai 93
Murakami, Takashi 203
music 8, 28, 30, 34, 39, 53, 75, 79, 81, 98, 174, 178, 209

New Look 27, 78, 85, 103
New York 8, 48–49, 54, 61, 70, 72, 86–87, 93, 142, 144, 177, 182, 184, 192, 206, 209, 232
Newson, Marc 169
Newton, Helmut 40
Nike 73
Nirvana 192

One Woman Show 138
open days 120
Organza Painted Lobster Dress 12
Orphism 11
Owens, Rick 216–31

Paris 8–9, 11–12, 21, 25, 27–28, 30, 32, 34, 44, 48–49, 61, 66–67, 70, 75,

78, 80, 83, 86–87, 93, 130, 134, 137, 142, 144, 148, 152, 166, 174, 178, 206, 216, 220
La Pauvrete de Luxe 24
People Tree 65
perfume 22, 28, 48, 67, 134, 138, 205
Pernet, Diane 38 ·
Perry Ellis 184, 192, 194, 206, 216
Perry Ellis Awards 184, 192, 206, 216, 234
Pescei, Sergei 38
pesticides 64
PETA (People for the Ethical Treatment of Animals) 62
photography 15, 22, 38–40, 61, 79–80, 84, 97–99, 134, 142, 169, 172, 174, 178
Picard, Jean-Jacques 172
Picasso, Pablo 21
Pisanello, Antonio 11
Poiret, Paul 21–22, 24, 78, 182
poor chic 24
Pop Art 15
Popova, Lyubov 12
portfolios 47–48, 120–22, 124, 126, 128
Portman, Natalie 184
Posen, Zac 182–91
Post-Hiroshima Look 34
postgraduates 118
power dressing 33, 67, 78, 103
PPR (Pinault-Printemps-Redoute) 47, 74
Prada 42, 47, 49, 70, 73, 84, 112, 174, 205
pre-collections 92
Première Vision 83, 86–88
Primark 64, 76
print studios 83
production calendar 90–91
promotion 15, 35, 38–39, 52, 54, 67, 92, 124–25, 182
proportion 27, 79, 97, 104–6, 110, 117, 122, 130, 151
publications 82
Pucci 46
Puma 47, 73–74
punks 8, 32, 34, 172, 177, 194
PVC 30

Quant, Mary 30

Rabanne, Paco 30
rag trade 44
Ramos, Luisel 61
ranges 112–13, 116
Raymond, Martin 81

ready-to-wear 15, 25, 28, 30, 35, 40, 48–49, 67, 69–70, 76, 86–87, 92, 96, 112, 138, 148, 203, 232, 234
Red Label 49, 73
Renaissance 11
research 79, 81, 84, 88, 90–91, 96–100, 102–3, 106, 109–10, 116, 122, 124, 138, 194
Reston, Ana Carolina 61
Revillon 216
Rhodes, Zandra 30, 32
Richemont 47
Rive Gauche 172, 174
Romans 8, 140
Rossi, Sergio 47
Russell, Peter 27
Russian Constructivists 12
Russian Doll 137
Rykiel, Sonia 50

Saab, Elie 67
Safari Chic 174
Saint Laurent, Yves 9, 15, 32, 34, 47, 172, 174
Salon European des Jeunes Stylistes 130
sample machinists 115, 117, 125–27
San Francisco 30, 232
Sander, Jil 47, 51, 74–75, 84, 103, 174
Sao Paulo 93
Saunders, Jonathan 126
Savile Row 75
Schiaparelli, Elsa 12, 38
Schneider, Stephan 169
Schwab, Mario 126
second-year projects 122
Sex and the City 54, 84, 118
Shanghai 93
Sherman, Cindy 38
shopping malls 6, 40, 44, 51, 128
shows 18, 30, 38, 40, 42, 55, 61, 75, 80, 84–92, 123, 126, 128
silhouette 11–12, 21–22, 25, 27, 30, 32, 61, 73, 75, 78–81, 85, 88–89, 91, 97, 102–4, 106, 110, 112–13, 117, 122, 130, 135, 137, 148, 160, 163, 174, 178, 184, 209, 232
Silver, Daniel 206, 209
Simms, David 40
Simons, Raf 40, 75
sketchbooks 103, 120
Slimane, Hedi 75, 172–81
slow fashion 65
Smith, Paul 75
Le Smoking 9, 172
Snoeren, Rolf 130

Credits

Snow, Carmel 85
sportswear 25, 27, 47, 49, 72–75, 78, 83, 206, 220, 232
spring/summer collections 6, 66, 70, 86–87, 90–92, 109, 135, 137–38
Sprouse, Stephen 203
Stars and Stripes 137
status 8, 49, 53, 62, 85, 135
Stepanova, Varvara 12
Stiebel, Victor 27
storyboards 100
style 6, 39, 53–54, 56, 70, 72, 75, 79, 84, 88
style tribes 8, 79, 81
styling 114–15, 172
stylists 6, 38, 40, 61, 84, 93, 117, 148
supermarket chic 76–77
Surrealism 12, 138
Swanson, Gloria 52
Swarovski 184, 234
sweatshops 64
Sydney 93
syllabus structure 121

Tag Heuer 46
tailoring 75
tattooing 8
Tear Dress 12
technology 6, 28, 72–74, 78, 81, 98, 107, 144, 163
teenagers 28, 56
television 6, 118
textiles 11, 21–22, 30, 32, 44, 73, 83, 97, 113, 122, 148, 182
third-year projects 122
Throup, Aitor 75
toiles 80, 88, 116–17
Tokyo 93, 216
Toledo, Ruben 38
Topshop 54, 56, 76
Toronto 206
trade fairs 83, 88–89, 252
trend agencies 82, 107
trend chasers 81–82
trends 6, 38–40, 49, 53, 65, 76–85, 88, 93

undergraduates 118
Ungaro, Emanuel 30
uniforms 8, 22, 24–25, 69, 194
universities 118–21
utility clothing 6
Utility Scheme 25

Valentino 67, 107
Van Beirendonck, Walter 35, 160–71
Van Noten, Dries 35, 160, 209

Van Saene, Dirk 35, 160, 169
Versace 49, 55, 70, 220
Vexed Generation 169
Vienna 11, 25
Viktor & Rolf 75, 130–39
Vionnet, Madeleine 24–25
Vogue 34, 39, 42, 84–85, 142, 148
Vuitton, Louis 33–34, 46, 49, 54, 84, 172, 203, 205

W.&L.T (Wild and Lethal Trash) 163
Walker, Catherine 118
Wall Street 47
Ward, Melanie 84
Warhol, Andy 15
waspie 27
Watanabe, Junya 152
websites 39, 42, 124, 163, 166, 250–53
welfare 58
Westwood, Vivienne 32, 118
Wet Look 30
Wiener Werkstätte 11
Willhelm, Bernhard 75, 123, 169
Williamson, Matthew 50
Wilson, Louise 121
Wintour, Anna 34, 85
Wode 144
Womenswear Designer of the Year Award 192
work experience 122, 125
workers' rights 64
workwear 6
Worth, Charles Frederick 21, 24–25, 66

Yamamoto, Yohji 33–34, 40, 75, 78, 84, 105, 148
Yee, Marina 35, 160
youth culture 8, 28, 98

Zara 76, 90
zeitgeist 78–85, 205
Zeitz, Jochen 74

3: Courtesy of Rick Owens. 7: Getty Images. Photo: Dave M. Bennett. 9: © WWD/Condé Nast/Corbis. 10: Catwalking.com. 12: © Condé Nast Archive/Corbis. Photo: Guy Marineau 14: AFP/Getty Images. Photo: Louisa Gouliamaki/Stringer. 16: AFP/Getty Images. Photo: Hugo Philpott. 18: AFP/Getty Images. Photo: Paolo Cocco. 19: AFP/Getty Images. Photo: Patrick Hertzog. 20: Time & Life Pictures/Getty Images. Photo: Paul Boyer. 23: Roger Viollet/Getty Images. Photo: Lipnitzki. 26: Time & Life Pictures/Getty Images. Photo: Gordon Parks. 29: Getty Images. Photo: Hulton Archive/Stringer. 31: © Bettmann/CORBIS. 32: © Condé Nast Archive/Corbis. 35: Catwalking.com. 36: AFP/Getty Images. Photo: Pierre Verdy. 37: Catwalking. com. 45: Bloomberg via Getty Images. 46: Getty Images. Photo: Robert Mora. 50: AFP/Getty Images. Photo: Yoshikazu Tsuno. 52: Getty Images. Photo: Apic. 55: WireImage. Photo: Jim Spellman. 56: AFP/Getty Images. Photo: Timothy A. Clary. 59: iStockphoto.com © Jessica Liu. 60 (top): Catwalking.com. 60 (bottom): Getty Images. 63: AFP/Getty Images. Photo: Steven Klein. 68: Getty Images. Photo: Andrew H. Walker. 71: AFP/Getty Images. Photo: Patrick Kovarik. 73: Catwalking.com. 74: Catwalking.com. 76: Bloomberg via Getty Images. 85: FilmMagic. Photo: Mike Coppola. 89: Sketch: Louise Henrikson. Photo: David Wise. 90: Photo: David Wise. 94–95: Catwalking.com. 97:

Photo: David Wise. 99: Photo: David Wise. 100–101: Photo: David Wise. 107: Photo: Kate Swingler. 111–116: Photo: David Wise. 117: Photo: Kate Swingler. 120–121: Photo: Kate Swingler. 124–125: Photo: David Wise. 127: Photo: David Wise. 129: Courtesy Marc Jacobs. 131: AFP/Getty Images. Photo: Pierre Verdy. 132: AFP/Getty Images. Photo: Jean-Pierre Muller. 133: AFP/Getty Images. Photo: Pierre Verdy. 134–135: Catwalking.com. 136: AFP/Getty Images. Photo: Pierre Verdy. 137: Catwalking.com. 139: AFP/Getty Images. Photo: Pierre Verdy. 140: Courtesy Boudicca. 143: Photo: Justin Smith. 144: AFP/Getty Images. Photo: Odd Andersen. 146–157: Catwalking.com. 158: AFP/Getty Images. Photo: Francois Guillot. 159: Getty Images. Photo: Chris Moore/Catwalking. 160–171: Courtesy Walter Van Beirendonck. 173: AFP/Getty Images. Photo: Olivier Laban-Mattei. 175 & 177: Photo: Hedi Slimane. 178-181: Courtesy Hedi Slimane. 182-191: Courtesy Zac Posen. 192-203: Courtesy Marc Jacobs. 204: AFP/Getty Images. Photo: Pierre Verdy. 205: Catwalking. com. 206-213: Courtesy Duckie Brown. Photo: Dan Lecca. 214: Getty Images. Photo: Frazer Harrison. 215: Getty Images. Photo: Frazer Harrison. 216-221: Photo: Owenscorp. 222: Photo: Oliver Zahm. 223-229: Photo: Owenscorp. 230: Photo: Oliver Zahm. 232-245: Courtesy Derek Lam.